The Pioneer History of Morgan County Ohio

The Pioneer History of Morgan County Ohio

JAMES M. GAYLORD

COMMONWEALTH BOOK COMPANY
St. Martin, Ohio

First Published in 1932
Copyright © 2016 by Commonwealth Book Company
All rights reserved. Printed in the United States of America

ISBN: 978-1-948986-29-8

Cover image: McConnellsville in 1846 as drawn by Henry Howe

The village of McConnelsville was laid out into streets, alleys and lots in the spring of 1817, by Gen. Robert McConnell, the proprietor. The proprietor then resided upon his farm in Muskingum county, and did not remove to the village for some years thereafter, where he died, leaving surviving him several daughters and one son, the late James A. McConnell.

The then town comprised only 92 lots and is known by owners and conveyors as the "Old Town." The "Old Town" is bounded on the north by the alley north of Liberty street; on the east by the alley east of East street; on the west by the alley west of West street, and on the south by the river. Some of the lots were sold by auction; the most of them by private sale. The first day of April, 1819, found the following families in the "Old Town," namely:

Jacob Kahler on lot No. 9; Moore & Paschal, lot No. 19; Jacob P. Springer, lot No. 28; Jonathan Porter, lot No. 35; John Williams, lot No. 51; Jacob Adams, lots Nos. 42, 44 and 57; Lewis Ramsey, lot No. 61; James Young, lot No. 64; Robert Robinson, lot No. 65; Philip Kahler, lot No. 66; Timothy Gaylord, lot No. 67; Jacob R. Price, lot No. 79; James Larison, lot No. 79.

Of the above list, Mr. Adams, who was then the head of the family, is the only survivor in 1873, when this is written. James Larison and James Young were the first tavern-keepers, holding forth in two-story hewed log houses, located on their lots. Mr. Larison for many years carried a weekly mail on horseback between Zanesville and McConnelsville, and no mail-carrier since that day has been as prompt in the performance of his duty as was Jimmy Larison.

Mr. Young was a brick-maker and layer, and for some time a justice of the peace. Jacob R. Price was the village blacksmith, and at one time was treasurer of the county. He removed with his children to Missouri, and died there.

Robert Robinson and Timothy Gaylord were the shoemakers, following their trade upon the lots where they resided. They were both residents for many years, and died in the village. The latter was the first county recorder and at one time held the office of county auditor and for several years was one of the justices of the peace.

Jacob Adams was the only merchant and trader at this date, keeping his store in a small frame building fronting the public square, where now stands the Seaman & Sons business establishment. He built the first brick house in the village and, perhaps, the only one then in the county, which he now occupies as a hotel. He was the postmaster of the village and so continued in and out for several years.

Jonathan Porter, Lewis Ramsey and Jacob Kahler were carpenters. the latter working some as a millwright. Mr. Porter was the first tax-collector, for in those days as in the present, the people were assessed and required to pay taxes.

Jacob P. Springer was the first

sheriff of the county, and at one time kept a tavern in the frame building upon his lot, No. 28, now occupied as a place of business by the McCarty's. He removed with his family to Muskingum county and died there not long since.

Philip Kahler was mostly engaged in the cultivation of corn, etc., upon the vacant lots and out-lots of the village.

Dr. S. A. Barker and Gen. Alex McConnell were single men and residents of the village. The first named was the only physician, was the first county clerk and the first schoolmaster. The doctor died some years since, leaving surviving him a widow, who now resides in the village.

Gen. McConnell had a tanyard, outside the "Old Town," afterwards in the northwest part of the present village, and boarded with Jacob Kahler. He died a few years since, leaving a widow (who is now a resident of the village) and a large family of children surviving. I am not aware of any other family, or any other adult other than those mentioned above who were residents of the village 54 years ago this present April. If there be any errors in the list of statements made I desire to be corrected. It may be of importance in the hereafter, if a Pioneer Association should ever be formed in the county.

All the pioneer settlers were blessed with several children. But few of the boys and girls of those days reside among us or are counted among the living masses. They are dead or have found homes in the far west, only a few living here.

Jacob Adams, Mrs. Jonathan Porter of Zanesville, H. H. Robinson of Butler county, Ohio, Mrs. James Lutton of Malta, James M. Gaylord, Mrs. George Russell, widow, of St. Louis, Mo., Andrew Kahler and Mrs. Ford Sill are the only persons known to me now surviving, who were residents of the village April 1st, 1819. There may be others, but they are not known to me.

Mrs. Ford Sill, Andrew Kahler, Jacob Adams and James M. Gaylord are the only living monuments within the present Morgan township and village of McConnelsville, surviving, the first day of April, 1873.

Mrs. Robert Robinson, deceased, was our first schoolmistress. Who is there now among us that can bring to mind the time when she so vigorously wielded the hickory rod over the backs and shoulders of the unruly youths of that day? Alas; they are all gone—silent or hushed up.

The school house of that period was a one-story log structure, and stood at the rear of the lot recently purchased by the county from Mr. Ford Sill. The lot then belonged to the county. The prevailing religious denominations were the Methodist, Presbyterian, Baptist, and a sprinkling of what were called New Lights. They worshipped for many years in the old court house, which was free for all comers and goers, and for every purpose, from the holding of the august tribunal of justice down to a bear show. The old court house stood on the lots where is now erected the present one. It was a two-storied brick, erected about the year 1820 or 1821, with the court room below and the public offices upstairs. James Young was the boss brickmaker and layer and Uncle Billy Fouts, now resident of Oregon (and father of Sol H. Fouts), was the boss carpenter. The only entrance to this model of a structure was on the side opposite Jacob Adams' tavern, and stood on a line with the public square, unprotected, without fence or shade trees, and all times was a fine and prominent mark to receive the peltings of the then young Arabs of the village. The glazier's bills were always paid by the county, and no questions asked.

The first court in the county was organized and held in a cabin upon lot No. 51, occupied by John Williams. The Seat of Justice was a carpenter's work bench upon which sat three associate judges of the county, the presiding judge failing to put in an appearance. The lawyers and suitors occupied a small area in front; the jury was packed in as small a compass as possible, at one side, and the spectators, witnesses, etc. (if not engaged in shooting at a mark, running horses, or in other sports and exercises), were huddled together in the very small vacancy allotted to them, or were peering through the door and other openings of the court house in the wilderness.

Mr. Nathan Dearborn, coroner of the county, was acting sheriff; Dr. Samuel A. Barker, clerk, and John Dolan, Esq., prosecuting attorney. The judges were Sherebiah Clark of Olive township, upon Duck Creek; William Reynolds of Brookville township, now Noble county, and William B. Young of Malta. All the officers of the first court, together with the persons composing the first grand and petit juries, are dead.

At the time of laying out the village of McConnelsville, there existed upon the present plat a growth of timber not exceeded in quantity, quality or size in any part of Ohio. The poplars, beeches, walnuts, hickories, sycamores, sugars, maples and other products of the forest, such as grapevines, spice wood, leather wood, paw paw, the pea vine, the great cattle feed of that day, were immense in growth and abundant in quantity, which when in cutting down, so encumbered the ground as to completely block up all the passage ways for both man and beast. Nothing could be done by our pioneers to get clear of the vast encumbrance, only by slow and laborious approaches. It all finally yielded to the ax and torch of the sturdy woodman, and now at this day scarcely a vestige of this immense and mighty forest is to be seen except perhaps in some antiquated building of that period, still existing and permitted to stand as a monument to the primeval days of the village.

McConnelsville in April, 1819, contained perhaps 75 inhabitants; one-third of them adults and two-thirds children. It has been asserted, and the assertion not contradicted, that no town in Ohio of its size and age can compete with McConnelsville in the production of children. This production may be attributed to its healthy location and to the general health of its people. Every year for the last 30 years the town and neighborhood had swarmed its hive of people, to supply the states and territories west of us with emigrants. Several families, together with many of its young men, have found homes and employment in all the states and territories between here and the Pacific ocean. It would be interesting to give a list of the families, together with the boys and girls, who were born and reared here, who have emigrated west. The list would be truly formidable, and would show, if investigated, a vast amount of wealth taken with them. Here among us, thru economy and "fair dealing" many fortunes have been made to be employed and enjoyed in other parts of the country.

Our town is constantly drained of much of its capital to be invested in better locations and more productive pursuits. This great flow of emigration and capital that is constantly going on from among us, may be attributed in part to the system of railroads prevailing in other sections of the country and all around us.

In railroad advantages and enterprise, we are wanting, and should the present state of affairs prevail, and be the rule forever, then we may make up our minds to continue as in the past, mere breeders of human beings to populate the other parts of the country.

In the early days of the village the people lived as all other people do who settle down in the wilderness. They were far away from the enjoyments, advantages and opportunities of the older settlements and of the present day. The river was their only thoroughfare, the keel boat, the perougee and the canoe were the only means of transportation. Roads, we had none, except bridle paths across the country from one neighbor and neighborhood to another. At the time, however, there was an important and very much traveled road leading from Marietta to Zanesville, and across the county through Center and Bristol townships, and so continued until the introduction of steamboats upon the river.

Zanesville was the only available point at that time where our grists were ground, except here and there through the country were erected horse mills, where the neighbors procured their corn meal.

"Hog and hominy," venison, bear, turkey, cornbread, spice and sassafras teas were the common table spread; but among the well-to-do families, "store coffee" or "Young Hyson," and wheat bread appeared on wash-days, or when we had company. In those days the people were truly kind and hospitable, and at all times ready and willing to assist each other in their labors to fell the forest, build the cabin and advance in the work of improvement. The political party spirit of the present day had no place or countenance among our people. Not until the great contest for the presidency in 1824, between Jackson, Clay, Adams and Crawford was it that our people were somewhat politically exorcised by the example set them by the outside barbarians. Newspapers were then but few, and not much read. A few copies of the Zanesville papers (Messenger and Express, or Gazette), and some other stray sheets, were procured and handed about among the villagers and perused with great interest and delight. On political, foreign, general and domestic news our people were kept pretty well posted, as far as it could be done by a mail once a week from Zanesville.

The village of Malta was our neighbor. Then, like it is at present, it thought itself a rival and would "put on airs" and pitch in. It was laid out by Messrs. Pool and Bell. The residents of Malta, in the year of April, 1819, were few and far between, strung along the river bank.

Judge W. B. Young, Jonathan Whitney, George Miller, John Seaman and William Palmer were the only families now remembered. Judge Young lived in what is now called Lower Malta, on the premises since occupied by his son, William B. Young, late deceased, and kept the first ferry across the river, between Malta and McConnelsville. George Miller kept tavern in a two-storied hewed log house on the lot and at the place where Mr. John Hall now keeps store. John Seaman was a shoemaker, following the business for many years upon the lot now occupied by the tobacco warehouse of Mr. Morris. Jonathan Whitney was a fisherman, living in a small cabin house upon the bank of the river, between the residences of Mr. Young and Mr. Miller.

Morgan township at that time was an original surveyed township, five by six miles, in which were located McConnelsville and Malta. Since that period the township has been divided, the river being the dividing line, and with annexations from adjoining townships, forms the now townships of Morgan and Malta.

In the township, upon the east side of the river, we find Isaac Hedges, T. M. Gates, Stephen Gates, William Fouts and Daniel Chandler, and perhaps the Scott boys, John, Obediah and Barney, or their father, living upon their farms, cultivating small patches. In the township west of the river, we find at this time, occupying their new-made entries, R. P. Stone, John Bell, Simeon Pool, Esq., Mr. Lucas and Samuel McCune, Sr., along the river. Out upon the hills, upon the new entries, we find the Johnsons, Alloways, Hugheses, Murpheys, Stevensons,

Shepards, Daweses, Beckwiths, and Benjamins. The two latter families settled upon Section No. 16. All of the above named persons, except Isaac Hedges and William Fouts, are believed to be dead.

In the location and establishment of the Seat of Justice for the new county of Morgan, there was much strife and contention among the rival sites. Malta had some pretensions, and put in its claim as the only suitable situation upon the river. It was urged upon the commissioners by some of the Maltaite lobbyists, that it was a very healthy village for no death had as yet occurred in the place, and that it was high and dry and beyond the reach of river floods; that McConnelsville, its rival, was a low, swampy and fever and aguish location, frequently subject to inundations, and as far inland as the foot of the hills, and that they had navigated with their canoes all over the town. These statements had no influence with the commissioners, however; and Malta, with its pretensions, subsided. Other places, interior, on the east side of the river, presented, and with much force and some influence, urged their respective claims. The strongest claim, interior, was that upon the farm of Mr. David Stevens, section No. 36, Bristol township. It was nearer the geographical center than any other, except the claim upon the farm now owned by Mr. Leland, in Bristol township, section No. 14, then owned by Mr. Chandler, of Muskingum county. Both of these sites were upon the much-traveled road leading from Marietta to Zanesville. The commissioners, E. Cutler of Washington county, and Mr. Lybrant of Pickaway county, in 1818, located the county seat at McConnelsville; Colonel David Robb, the other commissioner, dissented. The defeated parties then commenced a war against the new county seat, and got up a petition to the legislature asking the appointment of a new board of commissioners and a review of the proceedings. These petitions were so far respected as to procure, through the efforts of the member from Belmont county, the passage of a law in the House, designating new commissioners, with the power to review and re-locate.

The McConnelsvillians and their friends became alarmed at the turn things were taking before the legislature, and forthwith hastened with all their might to circumvent their opponents. No time was to be lost; in fact, they were sorely pressed for time. Word came that the law had passed the House and was then pending in the Senate.

A remonstrance was hastily gotten up, and to expedite the business the militia rolls in the hands of the captains of the state militia were consulted, and the names copied on the remonstrance. Mr. Jacob Adams, having the only good and unemployed horse in the village, mounted and started for Columbus across the country in great haste, following the bridle path through the wilderness by the way of Lancaster and reaching Columbus in the afternoon of the second day. Forthwith, Mr. Adams waited upon Colonel Jackson, then Senator from Muskingum county, who was the fast and tried friend of McConnelsville, and laid before him his ponderous roll of remonstrators against the passage of the bill.

Colonel Jackson had the bill called up in the Senate the next morning, and upon his motion, the bill was indefinitely postponed, only one senator voting in the negative. This action forever settled the county seat question for the new county of Morgan. It did not, however, produce harmony among all the people. Strife and opposition towards McConnelsville continued for some years thereafter, and not until that generation passed away did the animosity and hatred towards the village die out. On the waters of Duck Creek (which was then called a river by those who urged the county seat in that section), there were sites proposed; they being in the east end of the county and some distance from the center, were not seriously entertained by the commissioners.

As a bid and an inducement for the location of the county seat at McConnelsville, General Robert McConnell, the proprietor, proposed and entered into an agreement, making several donations of town lots and grounds for the use of the public, etc. Town lots, to-wit: Nos. 15, 22, 29 and 30, were donated upon which to erect county buildings. Lots Nos. 15 and 22 were afterwards sold by the county commissioners, No. 15 to Michael Devin and No. 22 to Thos. Devin. This sale was made for the purpose of raising money in the aid of the erection of the new court house and jail. Since the sale, lot No. 22 has been bought back by the commissioners from the late owner, Mr. F. Sill. Mr. D. H. Mortley now owns and occupies lot No. 15. On the rear of lot No. 22 and on the alley corner and but a short distance from the first town and school house, was built the first jail. It was an unique structure, its like, perhaps, never before or since has had an existence. A description of this, the first jail in Morgan county, would not be out of place. Out of the large poplars standing around its immediate vicinity, and longitudinally encumbering the earth in every direction, the county commissioners had built the first prison. The logs used in this structure were from 18 to 24 inches in diameter, scutched down on the inside so as to make an even and smooth surface, the bark taken off and the logs notched down at the corners, making the room almost air-tight. A ponderous door, three inches thick, made of oak plank, driven full of nails and spikes, was hung in an opening made in one end. The structure when completed was 12 feet square, with the floor and the ceiling made from large hewed logs, and when finished it was locked up and the key delivered by the contractor to the county commissioners.

This model of a prison was never opened for the confinement of anyone. It seemed to be a terror to all evil-doers. On account of its size, construction and location, it was voted a failure and in a short time was entirely abandoned; the lot upon which it stood having passed to Thomas Devin, by sale from the commissioners. The county commissioners of that day, and who were the first, and under whose supervision the first jail was built, were John Shutt of Deerfield, Richard Cheadle of Windsor, and Wm. Montgomery of Bloom.

Jail building with these men was a new business, and besides being limited in their means and materials, much allowance must be made for them in their first effort.

Horse thieves, counterfeiters, and other criminals becoming quite plenty in the county of Morgan; the county commissioners undertook the erection of another more substantial, commodious and safe prison house for the reception and safekeeping of such outlaws and also of debtors; for in those days, in Ohio, it was quite common to have the jails full of debtors.

The heathenish policy of imprisoning one for a debt he could not pay, has long since been abolished, and now is no longer held as a crime, deserving punishment by incarceration within prison walls.

This structure, built as the second jail in the county, deserves some notice, showing the improvement made on jail No. 1. It was erected on the rear of the lots upon which the present public buildings now stand. It was built out of hewed poplar logs about twelve inches square, neatly and closely fitting together, with an inner wooded wall made of like material and size as the outer, fitting together in the same manner, with a space of one foot between the two walls, filled with stone, making a good solid wall of about three feet thick; two rooms with an entry or hall of six feet between them. The rooms were about 15 feet square, with heavy and well nailed doors, one on the out entrance and two inside, leading into the rooms, with iron-grated windows for light and ventilation; small square apertures were made in each partition wall, through which the sheriff or jailer passed the rations to the inmates. It was secure in every part except in the ceilings—there were its weak points. This jail for many years answered the purpose, but like all jails, even of more modern construction, was not altogether proof against escapes, for the jail deliveries were frequent and annoying to the officers and keepers.

A few years before the demolition of the old court house, jail No. 2 gave way to the erection of the present No. 3. No one now claims to be the planner of the present No. 3 miserable and badly constructed prison. From the old jail several burglars, horse thieves, counterfeiters and murderers were sent to serve a term of years in the Ohio penitentiary.

General McConnel, the proprietor, also donated for the use of the county (not the village, as some may suppose) two squares, or five acres, including streets and alleys, for parade grounds. Also, to the Presbyterian denomination, two lots, Nos. 1 and 2 in the Second Addition; also Lots Nos. 13 and 14 to the Friends, or Quakers, now owned and occupied as a residence by E. M. Stanbery, Esq. Also two lots to the regular Baptist church, north side of Jefferson between Main and West streets. Also to the Methodist church two lots. Nos. 11 and 12, in the Second Addition. Also, lots for school house purposes were donated and located in different parts of the village. Also, a portion of the present burial ground was a donation from the proprietor.

The greater part of the present burial ground was a donation made by T. M. Gates, Esq., out of his tract below and adjoining the village. These burial ground donations were made to the county.

Several of these donations were not located by the proprietor when made, nor for some years thereafter, for the reason that they were not required for the purpose designated, but when called for they were promptly made and duly transferred. The Quaker and Baptist lots have never been used for the purpose for which they were appropriated, but have been diverted to other and different uses.

If my recollection serves me, McConnel also made a donation of ground, somewhere in the village, for a market place.

It will be observed that the donations to secure the county seat at this place were ample and liberal for the purposes intended, amounting in the aggregate to almost 30 town lots and, at that day, worth at least $5000. All these donations are now of great value. The most of them have been improved and in that way have added much to the favorable appearance of the village. No one at this day should enter complaint against the proprietor on the score of illiberality. The proprietor was not only liberal in the above gifts, but, for many years after the settling of the village, the inhabitants enjoyed a free range all over the proprietor's possessions, in the article of firewood, of timber, stone and other materials used in the construction of their dwellings, barns, stables, fences, etc. In fact, in his absence, there was no limit to their trespasses. They pitched in without restraint and enjoyed the spoils while they lasted.

After the proprietor came to live with us, he, to some extent, put down the brakes upon the wholesale piracies committed on his domains, but he showed great public spirit in the erection of buildings, improving of roads, and clearing up the forest. At a great outlay of capital, he built a dam across the river and erected a lock therein for the passage of boats, and improved the site with a grist mill and factories, and so continued in the good work of improving and building up the village until the day of his death, which was on the 3rd of August, 1841.

Reminiscences of the court of common pleas of this county may be interesting to the younger and bring back to the memory of the older people, events long since forgotten.

The records of the court are still preserved in the clerk's office and show that on the 6th day of April, 1819, was held the first court at McConnelsville. The court convened in a log building located on lot No. 51, now occupied by Mrs. Jonas Powell, then owned by John Williams, and on the alley corner thereof, fronting Main street.

Ezra Osborn, Esq., then a resident of Portsmouth, was the presiding judge of the judicial circuit. Judge Osborn did not find his way over to Morgan county until the following March.

Owing to the physical structure of the judge about the head, neck and shoulders, the lawyers upon the circuit nicknamed him "Judge Spud." In that day, one president and three associate judges constituted the common pleas court. These judges were elected by the legislature and for the term of seven years. The presiding judge was supposed to be learned in the law. He must, therefore, be a lawyer.

The associates were generally honest, substantial gentlemen, of sound judgment and good appearance, of fair ability and of general information without prejudice, hatred or ill-will towards any one.

In some instances, however, there were failures in all or part of these important qualifications. If there should be any such, it was set down to a mistake by the judge-makers, and patiently borne with, for in those days impeachment was but seldom resorted to.

The wags about the court house and the court room would have their fun at the expense of the honorable judiciary and at times indulged in pretty rough remarks. They would declare there were 1000 judges upon the bench, instead of four, the number designated and authorized by the constitution. To come at this arithmetical conclusion they made the president judge to represent the figure one, and the three associate judges were merely three ciphers, add to the right hand.

This contempt and want of confidence in the construction and organization of our court, prevailing at that day, in time brought upon the state the present expensive and inefficient judicial system we now labor under, and to reform which a constitutional convention has been called.

In the absence of Judge Osborn, the organization of the court devolved upon the three associates, viz: Wm. Runnels, Sherbiah Clark and Wm. B. Young. Wm. Runnels acted as president judge, and signed the journals and records of the court, and to whom the attorneys addressed themselves when presenting their motions, law points and exceptions.

It is said that there were seldom appeals taken or errors signed and filed against the decisions or opinions of these judges. It was not until after the appearance of the president judge upon the bench, when one lawyer meets another, that there arose differences of opinion.

At the organization of the first court in the county there were no resident lawyers. In fact, at that time, we were destitute in the village of both lawyers and preachers; we had but one doctor. In the way of preaching our people depended upon the itinerancy. The attorneys practicing at our log cabin bar, at this early day, were residents of Zanesville, and were S. W. Culbertson, General Herrick, C. B. Goddard, Willis Silaman, A. Downer, John Dolan, Alex Harper and Richard Stillwell.

Silaman, Goddard, Harper and Stillwell afterward became somewhat distinguished as lawyers and politicians in Ohio. All the early lawyers visiting the bar of this county are now deceased. John Doland, Esq., without his family, became the first resident lawyer and put out his sign notifying the contentious that he was "an attorney and counsellor at law, and solicitor in chancery, in Morgan and adjoining counties."

For want of constant employment as an attorney and pettifogger, Dolan engaged himself in keeping school in the log cabin house upon lot No. 66. Some few years after the organization of the county, Judge John E. Hanna became a resident attorney, and soon after him, James L. Gage, Esq. Judge Hanna still resides in the village. Mr. Gage emigrated west and a few years since died in Illinois. Other lawyers, in time, followed these pioneer attorneys, flickered with their rushlights for a short time, among us, then went out or emigrated west.

The law business, like all other kinds of professions and businesses, cannot flourish or be made profitable without the necessary capital, therefore, failures must sometimes take place.

No business appears to have been done by the court on the first day of the term. On the second day of the term, April 6th, 1819, the associate judges appointed Dr. Samuel A. Barker, clerk of the court; John Donald, Esq., prosecuting attorney; Timothy Gaylord, county recorder; and Wm. Davis of Windsor township, county surveyor. The first judgment entered by the court was in favor of General Isaac Van Horn of Zanesville against John Dodds, and for the sum of $114.34 and his costs.

At a called court held May 20th, 1819, the first letters of administration were granted Dr. Samuel Martin upon the estate of his brother, Thomas Martin, deceased. Dr. Samuel Martin now resides in Zanesville. His brother, Thomas Martin, was drowned in crossing the Muskingum river a few miles above the village. The Martins, Samuel, Thomas and George, were Englishmen, and had landed in the county only a short time before the death befalling their brother.

The second regular term of court was held on the 5th day of July, 1819, in a cabin house upon lot No. 19 now occupied by Mrs. Allison. Nathan Dearborn, of Windsor township, father of Perkins L. Dearborn, of Meigsville township, was the coroner and acting sheriff of the county (there being no sheriff elected yet). Coroner Dearborn then summoned and returned the following named gentlemen as the first grand jury of the county, namely: William M. Dawes who was appointed foreman by the court, Sylvanus Newton, Jas. Deveraux, A. Devol, Zadock Dickerson, Gilbert Olney, Isaac Hedges, Simeon Morguridge, Samuel Henery, Asa Emerson, Nathaniel Shepard, Rufus P. Stone, Alex McConnel, Archipaid McCollum and Richard Cheadle, all of whom are deceased except Isaac Hedges, who, much respected and at a good old age, resides in Meigsville township. This first grand jury of the county would, in ability and in the absence of "malice, hatred or ill-will towards anyone, and without fear, favor or affection, or reward or hope thereof" favorably compare with any other grand jury ever impaneled in the county. At that day the court had authority to grant license to keep tavern, etc., to those who were suitable persons, and had the necessary accommodations and fixtures about them for the entertainment of man and beast. James Young's was the first licensed tavern, which was kept by him in McConnelsville on the lot occupied by Watkins and Roland. He was licensed for one year, and required to pay the sum of $7.00 therefor. Young's tavern was a one and a half story hewed log house with two rooms below and a like number above. One of the lower rooms was used as the kitchen and dining room, and the other was the parlor, sitting, baggage and bar-room; the upper rooms were sleeping apartments. This was the crack hotel of the place at this period, where all the lawyers, judges, suitors, witnesses, etc. (after the fashions of the times) rested themselves. It is apparent that some little progress has been made in the hotel line about here in the last 54 years.

Jacob P. Springer, who was the first sheriff of the county, took out a license at this time to keep tavern. It was kept in the frame building by him built upon the lot where the McCartys do business. It was, in every particular, held to be an improvement to Young's pretension for a tavern. On the 7th day of July, 1819, the court ordered an election to be held on the 17th day of July, 1819, in the new township of Center, for the election of two justices of the peace.

The first indictment presented by the grand jury was against Enoch Loper for an assault and battery upon the body of one James Frisby who (Frisby) afterwards became a justice of the peace and a leading and influential character in the township of Bloom. He emigrated somewhere west, and there died some years since. To this indictment Loper plead not guilty, and the first petit jury of the county was called and impaneled and sworn, composed of the following named persons: T. M. Gates, Benj. Johnson, W. Murphy, Wm. Lewis, Micha Adams, Philip Kahler, Benjamin Williams, Elijah Williams, Abraham Hews, John Seaman, Samuel White and B. W. Talbott. The jury retired outside the log cabin court house, under the charge and watch of a sworn officer, who was "not to permit the jury to have anything to eat or drink (water excepted) until they agreed upon a verdict." The jury soon agreed upon a verdict, and came into court and reported that they found the said Loper guilty. The court assessed a fine of $3.00 and costs of prosecution. The court granted to Jacob Adams a license to vend goods in McConnelsville, which was the first, and at that time the only store in Morgan county, for which Mr. Adams was required to pay $20.00.

July 17th, 1819, the court ordered elections to be held in the new townships of Bloom, York, Penn and Bristol, on the 24th day of July, 1819, for two justices of the peace in each, the Bloom election to be held at the house of James Whitaker; York at the house of Michael Stoneburner; Penn at the house of Isaac Harris, Sr., and for Bristol at the house of Simon Merwin. Geo. Miller made application for and procured a license to keep the first tavern in Malta.

At the October term, 1819, held October 4th, James Reed was the first person naturalized in the court. Mr. Reed was a native of Ireland, and resided on Duck Creek, now Noble county. The first slander suit in Morgan county common pleas court was tried on the 4th of October, 1819 Ezekiel Hyatt, plaintiff, vs. Philip Moore, defendant. Hyatt charged Moore with having sworn to a lie on a trial of a case before a justice of the peace.

The jury which tried the case was composed of the following gentlemen, viz: Levi Davis, John B. Perry, Phineas Coburn, Simeon Blake, Jas. Whitaker, William Silvey, James Harris, Jared Andrews, Levi Ellis, Levi Deaver, John Shutt and Jonathan Porter. The jury found that the defendant Moore did falsely, maliciously, etc., defame the good name, fame and reputation of the defendant Hyatt and assessed his damages at only $17.00. In those days they would slander one another, but in the opinion of a very respectable jury of 12 men, the slandered person was not considered much damaged in his character, by the false and malicious utterances of the slanderer. This practice and rule of light verdicts in slander suits prevail at this day.

The grand jury at the March term of 1820, Ezra Osborn presiding, found only two bills of indictment: one against Mr. Enoch Loper for assault and battery upon the body of one John Hull, and one against John Hull for assault and battery upon the body of Enoch Loper. Hull entered a plea of guilty and was fined one dollar and costs. In the case of Enoch Loper, the prosecuting attorney, John Dolan, Esq., who seemed to have become disgusted with the manner in which justice was being administered by the court, suggested that a nolli prosequi be entered upon the Loper indictment; thereupon Dolan resigned, and Richard Stillwell, Esq., was appointed in his stead.

From the frequency in which Loper's name appears upon the court records, we take it that on all public occasions he was inclined to be quarrelsome and contentious, particularly when well primed with the aqua vitae of that period which was plenty and cheap, and handed around and freely imbibed in at all public gatherings and by nearly all of our people. At these gatherings it was the fashion to bring up and settle questions of differences and veracity between men, by a resort to the fist, foot, teeth and thumb—thumping, kicking, biting and gouging one another. At this term a license was granted to Edwin Corner & Co. to vend goods, for which they paid $20.00. This store was kept in a small frame building upon the lot now occupied by the McCartys. At this term of court. Jacob P. Springer was sworn in and gave bond, he being the first sheriff of Morgan county.

But few of the men who, at that early period, participated in the busy scenes of public life and in the pioneer organization of the county and the court, are alive.

In the term of 54 years finds but few of the actors of that period among us. Of all the persons named in the above recollections and proceedings we recognize as now living only Dr. Samuel Martin, Isaac Hedges, Jacob Adams, Edwin Corner and John E. Hanna. Messrs. Adams, Hedges and Hanna are residents of the county; the other two, Martin and Corner, live in other parts of the state, quite old and infirm.

Of the 39 persons composing the first grand jury and the two petit juries of the county, only one now survives, viz, Isaac Hedges.

Reference to old time documents, containing facts in the past history of the county, may be interesting to some, if not all, of our people. The political history of our county, if looked up, would furnish several chapters full of incidents, anecdotes and interesting facts. I have been looking into some of the records of the past, and find that the first election held in this county was in October, 1819, and for county officers only, namely: Three commissioners, a sheriff and a coroner. The abstract of this election is on file in the clerk's office, and was made out and certified to by Samuel A. Barker, the clerk; W. B. Young, associate judge, and James Young, justice of the peace on the 18th day of October; 1819. The township poll books of this election are not among the files in the clerk's office. If these books could be found they would furnish a pretty full list of the early male settlers of the county.

The persons voted for at this election for county commissioners were Wm. Montgomery of Bloom township, who received 323 votes; Richard Cheadle of Windsor township, 303 votes; and John Shutt of Deerfield township, 318 votes, and were declared elected. For the same office, David Fulton had 200 votes; Sylvanus Piper, 252; Robert McKee, 257; Enoch McIntosh, 22; William Craig and John Spears, 11 votes each, and A. Wharton, 13.

For sheriff, J. P. Springer received 289; B. W. Talbott, 220; and Nathan Dearborn, 60.

For coroner, Sylvanus Olney had 243; Thomas Devin, 227; and James Young, 58. Of all this list of candidates, Enoch S. McIntosh, Esq., of Beverly, Washington county, is the only one known to be living. The number of votes cast at this election was about 653. Morgan township, then including the territory of the present Malta township, gave at this election, 80 votes. A half century afterwards the same territory can give near 1000 votes.

The successful candidates for commissioners in Morgan township each had 67 votes, and their opponents only 13—showing the feeling then prevailing and governing the voters in this location. This election was merely local and held for the purpose of electing certain county officials. There seems to have been none of those political questions and issues, so prominent in after days, involved in this election.

The question then agitating our pioneer settlers brought out a full vote in all parts of the county and was the "East End" of the county against the "West End" and Center, and upon the county seat question.

The county seat had been located in the spring of that year at McConnelsville by the commissioners appointed by the legislature for that purpose. Nearly all the votes in the east part of the county, including Meigsville and a part of Bristol, were bitterly hostile to the location at McConnelsville, and determined to upset it if possible.

The opponents of McConnelsville appeared in all their strength at this election for county commissioners. In the issue the "East End" was defeated by a majority of about 60. This result was quite encouraging and induced them to make another effort before the legislature for the removal of the county seat. They went to work, and in the following December presented their petitions before the legislature praying for the appointment of other commissioners to review and relocate the county seat. In a former part of these Reminiscences I have related the manner, the ways and the means resorted to by the remonstrators to defeat this, the last effort of the petitioners.

The "East .Enders" gave up the contest and yielded as gracefully as possible to the shrewd management and muster rolls of the "West Enders" and McConnelsvillians.

The abstract before me of this election, Center, Brookfield, Noble, Olive, and Olive Green were unanimous in their opposition to the election of the successful candidates for commissioners. Meigsville and Seneca were nearly so, and Bristol, one-third. How Seneca township, now in Guernsey county, became a part of Morgan county, and how afterwards it was lost to us, is not explained by any records yet found.

At that election, Olive Green, now Jackson township, Noble county, gave an unanimous vote for Fulton, Piper and McKee for commissioners, and, what is remarkable, they continued a unit at all elections up to the presidential election in 1828. It was supposed that at the presidential election of that year every voter in the township was a friend to General Jackson and would cast him his vote. The following anecdote is related, going to show the ways, means and expedients resorted to by the Jacksonians of Olive Green township to manifest that unity so much desired at the presidential election in 1828. Before the polls were opened on the day of election, it was resolved by those present that the vote then about to be cast should be unanimous for Jackson, and all negative votes, should any appear, should be held as fraudulent, and not counted. The voting then commenced and everything appeared to be going on satisfactorily for the Jacksonians until the tickets were counted out; then it was discovered that there was one ballot in the box for John Q. Adams. The deceit and treachery of an independent voter was so glaring that the clamor and indignation of the Jacksonians became unbounded. On the suggestion of the cheated voters the judges of elections declared the ballot a fraud, and refused to have the vote counted and returned. Thus the poll book showed the vote in this township in 1828, for president, 31 votes for Jackson and none for Adams. At the next annual election thereafter the fraudulent voter who, in the meantime, had been found out and "spotted," made his appearance at the polls and offered his ballot. He was challenged for cause and also demanded to show his ticket before he could vote. This demand he refused to comply with and, fearing trouble if he remained among the excited bystanders, he left the place "on double quick." One of the judges, fleet upon foot, seized the ballot box and, with a Jackson ticket in his hand, gave chase after the fugitive voter, who had penetrated far into the forest. After a long chase he came up with the recusant voter and demanded he should vote the ticket of the majority, and thrust upon him "the ticket" and insisted that the trembling free man should place it in the box. The voter hesitated, parleyed, shuffled about, and at length yielded to the pressure and consented to vote. But, lo and behold, to the astonishment of all present, there appeared, in the count of the ballot, that same opposition vote.

This anecdote was told at the time the events were fresh, to show the sentiments and the proceedings of our pioneer people in the manner in which elections were held and conducted. I will not vouch for the full truth of the story. There is no doubt, however, that something of the kind did take place down in Jackson township in those early days.

The men of Jackson township, who in those early days went into the wilderness and caused it to bud and blossom and present at this day well improved farms, and who acted together with such unanimity, were the Carrels, Hugheses, Keiths, Lowes, Oliphants, Stevenses, Taylors, Ratliffs, Roaches and Wallers. They were mighty men, yet unlettered and unlearned; they were honest, industrious, generous and reliable. They were plain-spoken, determined men, despising treachery and double-dealing, visiting always the offender with punishment and treatment commensurate with the offense. They were so unanimous in their political sentiments and actions, and having unbounded confidence in the honesty, integrity and moral worth of "Old Hickory" that, some years since, they petitioned the proper authorities and caused the name of their township to be changed from that of Olive Green to that of Jackson. But the stranger came among them and, with his smooth, oily tongue and fanatical political notions, disturbed their peace and harmony, broke up their unanimity, so that in these degenerate days Jackson cannot be said to be a unit in thought and political action.

The first election we have record of held in Morgan township for a justice of the peace was the 3rd day of July, 1819, Alex. McConnell, Daniel Chandler and John Pettit, judges, and Jesse L. Pasehall and Simon Pool, Jr., clerks. Thirty-six votes were cast. I here give their names to show to the present generation who it was that stood about the polls and were interested in elections more than a half century ago, namely: Lewis Ramey, Gilbert Olney, Nathaniel Sprague, William M. Dawes, Amasa Piper, Sylvanus Piper, J. Bell, Alexander McConnell, Simon Pool, Jacob Adams, Joseph Smith, William Lewis, Jacob R. Price, John Pettit, Robert Aikins, Sr., John Smith, William Hughes, John Williams, Philip Kahler, John Seaman, Abraham Hughes, Benj. T. Johnson, Isaac Walbridge, Timothy M. Gates, W. C. Johnson, Israel Redmond, Jonathan McMullen, William Murphy, James Larrison, Nathaniel Shepard, James A. Young, Samuel A. Barker, Jonas Fox, Charles Brian and Henry Aumiller.

Of this list of pioneer voters, Jacob Adams and Charles Brian are the only survivors. This election was held for one justice of the peace.

The turn-out seems to have been small and Timothy M. Gates was elected, having received fifteen votes, the other candidates being Isaac Walbridge, Nathaniel Shepard, and William Hughes.

It will be noticed that two of the officers of this election refused or neglected to vote, or at least their names do not appear upon the list of voters. At this late date, it would be difficult to assign the reason for their neglect, unless it might have been that, under the influence of the frequent potations of stimulants, they found themselves under the table, and thereby were prevented from exercising the elective franchise and independence then guaranteed to all white male inhabitants by the then constitution of the state.

In those days it was the fashion everywhere at elections for candidates to treat their friends and also their enemies to extend merely a "smell." Liberally and frequently they indulged the generosity of the candidates during the day. It was common at the election stand to find the "big bellied bottle" exhibited and set out with the name of the candidate inscribed thereon.

It was the order of the day, to first vote and then drink the success of the favorite candidate from his bottle. If any candidate should have conscientious scruples about furnishing his demijohn, well-filled, his chances for success were slim on that day. This being the rule, rigidly observed and enforced, the officers of election, like many of the outsiders, would become quite mellow and overcome before the closing of and counting out of the polls. But they being men of very strong nerves and constitutions, and withal, ambitious, they admirably managed some way to weather through, and make out a tolerably legible report of their proceedings. In those days, it was none of the fiery, untamed benzine and needle-gun whiskey that was imbibed by the voters and officers. It was the pure corn and rye without adulteration by "foreign ingredients."

McConnelsville in the last fifty-four years has propagated and sent out into the wide world more boys perhaps than any other town of its age and size in the state. Malta, its neighbor, has not in this period of time been idle. McConnelsville and Malta boys may be found in every state and territory west of us; they may be found, in some way peculiar to themselves, battling for a competence, for wealth, for distinction, or for honor. A number of them have gone to that bourne from whence no traveler returns; many of them have taken the advice of good old Horace Greeley and "gone west," and not a few still remained among us, hanging on to the willows, Macauber-like "waiting for something to turn up."

We remember the following-named boys—big and little—who were here in McConnelsville and Malta in 1820: Andrew and William Kahler, sons of Jacob Kahler; Silas Kahler, son of Philip Kahler; Robert O. Porter, son of Jonathan Porter; John, David and Samuel Williams, sons of John Williams; Eli S., John H., James T. and Worley Adams, son of Jacob Adams; Elias Ramey, son of Lewis Ramey; David, Peter and William Young, sons of James Young; H. H. Robinson, son of Robert Robinson; James M. and John M. Gaylord, sons of Timothy Gaylord; Thomas, James and Abel Larrison, sons of James Larrison; Alexander R., Amzi C., Robert A., David C. and Henry R. Pinkerton, sons of Alexander R. Pinkerton; Elias, Charles and Horatio Gates, sons of Timothy M. Gates; William Collison, son of John Collison; Robert and Jesse Winter, sons of Robert Winter; W. W. McGrath, nephew of Edwin Corner.

In Malta: William B. Alexander, and Joseph Young, sons of Judge Young; William and Matthew Miller, sons of George Miller; Milton, Harmon, Henry and Chas. O. Seaman, sons of Simon Pool; J. R. Bell, son of John Bell; Alexander, Ambrose and William Palmer, sons of W. Palmer, and James Van Horn, son of W. Van Horn. There may be other names to be added to this 1820 list, but they do not occur.

About the year 1820, our local politicians, dropping the national party distinctions of that day, were divided into and called "Brimstones" and "Juntos." The "Juntos" were the self constituted and an organized office-seeking and office-holding ring or cabal, claiming and clamoring for all the offices, both big and little. In all their meetings and proceedings they were secret. They were vindictive, intolerant and proscriptive towards their watchers, the "Brimstones." The "Brimstones," not so numerous as the "Juntos," being proscribed from the enjoyment of political power and place, were the bitter and uncompromising enemies of the "Juntos." The "Brimstones" received their sulphurious name from the then existing fact that the itch prevailed to some perceivable and demonstrative extent among some of the members of the party and their families. The leader of the "Junto" party was one Jonathan Williams, a carpenter and house-joiner, who, in 1820, emigrated to our village from Baltimore. He possessed some talent, great energy, and no little courage; in fact he was a Baltimore City Rough, whom the "Brimstones" reported and charged, had left Baltimore for Baltimore's good. Williams was an intense hater, and ready and willing to participate in all rows, riots and fights in the village and neighborhood and seemed to be put forward fully armed, and, on all occasions wielded a crooked, knotty, lignum-vitae stick about 18 inches long, with which he rushed in and flourished to the dismay of all his opponents. The stick he named the "Old Presbyterian." Williams rusticated here, in the wilderness, some two or three years, worked some at his trade, got married, purchased a tract of land, now owned by D. C. Blonden and Joseph Smith, for a country residence, naming it "Wyandot."

He was for a short time the first auditor of the county, and on account of family dissensions and difficulties, left our village for the South and died in New Orleans. Before he left he bestowed the "Old Presbyterian" upon his friend, Neri Shugart. "Old Uncle Neri" preserved the fighting emblem up to the time of his death. Since his death the "Old Presbyterian" has not been seen, and among the old pioneers entirely forgotten. It should have been preserved; it would have been an appropriate relic to deposit in a home museum as an attacking and defensive emblem of olden times.

For the want of a better one, T. M. Gates was recognized as the leader of the "Brimstones." He was, however, no match for the pugilistic, vigilant and dashing Williams. The "Juntos" so admirably managed local political matters as to always come out first best in nearly every contest. They took special pains to secure the favor and suffrage of a majority of newcomers as soon as they landed in the county, and thus managed to command the situation. The presidential contest in 1824 between Jackson, Adams, Clay and Crawford, coming on, somewhat disconcerted these local parties. Afterwards at the presidential contest in 1828, between Jackson and Adams, "Brimstones" and "Juntos" were entirely lost sight of and the individuals comprising these parties became divided and disorganized, commingling the "Brimstones" with the "Juntos" and the "Juntos" with the "Brimstones." The political past with these men was forgotten, or held as bygones and men who had been implacable enemies in the last local political organization came together, embraced, became the fast, noisy and active friends of either the "Hero of New Orleans" or the "Duke of Braintree." From 1828, forward to this day, the national party distinctions have been recognized and adopted, the old "Brimstone" and "Junto" parties, with now but few survivors in the county being almost entirely forgotten and only alluded to as a fact in our past political history.

In 1819, an incident took place somewhere upon Wolf Creek, in its excitements and escapes almost or quite equal to the famous Putnam wolf story, and its relation at this day is thought worthy of a place in these Reminiscences.

Abe and Bill Hews, well known characters, then residents of Morgan township, now Malta, were famous hunters. To hunt the bear, the wolf and other ferocious animals infesting our woods at that time was their favorite sport and a great source of profit. All along Wolf Creek and its waters the ferocious wolf had its den or place of concealment and safety. The creek derived its name from the great number of wolves prowling and depredating in that region.

At that day the treasurer of the county paid $3.00 for each wolf scalp taken and presented. This was something of an inducement to Abe and Bill to lay down the shovel and the hoe and go forth with their trusty rifles in the pursuit and capture of the great enemy of the sheep and hog families.

In one of their hunting excursions, they tracked a she wolf to her den. Arrived at the entrance, Abe proposed to Bill to crawl in after the wolf. Bill declined the job, not like Putnam's negro, for want of courage, for he was as brave as Julius Caesar, but suggested that as Abe was the smaller man, he had better penetrate the den, whilst he (Bill) would stand watch at the entrance and despatch the wolf as she emerged from her retreat. Abe to some extent disrobed himself and entered the den, cautiously making his way towards the lair of the inmate and her pups. On the approach of Abe, the old wolf seemed to comprehend the situation of things and made a spring towards Abe in order to pass him and egress herself into the outside freedom and light. In making the passage, the wolf and Abe met in a compressed part of the passage-

way. Then it was that Abe got the worst of the adventure. She tore and lacerated Abe's body and buckskins in a terrible manner. Bill, true to his trust and responsibility, stood at the entrance with his faithful and trusty rifle in hand, and as she emerged shot the old wolf dead.

Abe, not to be defeated in his adventure and prospective profit, advanced to the lair and brought the young wolves forth. The scalps of the old and young wolves brought into the purses of Abe and Bill quite a sum of money for those days. These men, from the great flow of immigration into the county, becoming somewhat cramped for hunting territory and the wild game becoming scarce and unreliable as a source of subsistence and profit, pulled up stakes like Lo, and departed from their familiar hunting grounds to find, in the far west, a more congenial people, more freedom and more game.

On Christmas day in 1829 a somewhat exciting election took place at the court house in McConnelsville. It was held for the purpose of electing three trustees and a treasurer, to manage the affairs of School Section Sixteen, of the original surveyed township No. 10, in Range 12. The township of Morgan then contained Malta township, too, and was the election district. Samuel Barker, Sr., John Jack and Guy Benjamin were the judges, and James L. Gage and Dr. Edward Dawes were the clerks of the election. The number of voters at that election were certified to be 36. I here give the names, showing who took part in this election who now survive, namely: Richard Gildersleeve, Guy Benjamin, J. Seaman, John Christy, Jacob Johnson, J. Arthur, Samuel A. Barker, John W. Johnson, William Hawkins, Richard McKibben, Michael Wiseman, W. C. Shugert, J. Kirk, John E. Hanna, John Kelsey, John R. Robinson, Wm. Pettit, Joseph Price, David Newman, W. R. Allen, James L. Gage, Alex. Simpson, Samuel Baker, W. Dawes, Neri Shugart, Joseph Skinner, S. Welch, Benj. Nott, Timothy Gaylord, M. Devin, Levi G. Wells, Benj. Beckwith, J. Baker, A. McKee, Sam T. Clymer, Robt. McConnell, Edwin Corner, A. D. Hanson, Jacob Adams, P. Kahler, John Jack, David Evans, S. F. Gates, J. R. Price, Thos. Devin, F. A. Barker, Charles Robertson, R. A. Pinkerton, Edward Dawes, John Bell, Luther D. Barker, E. Odgen, John Lansley, E. Baker, John H. Stone, David Young, Isaac Williams, Jesse Conway, P. B. Johnson, Zuriel Sherwood, Robert Robinson, M. Michael, William Durbin, J. Pettit, Jonathan Porter, James Nulton.

For trustees, Michael Wiseman received 37 votes, William Durbin, 35, John E. Hanna, 34, James Baker, 31, John W. Johnson, 31, William Ball, 28, Elijah Ball, 1.

For treasurer, James E. Marquis got 33 votes, Henry Dawes, 31, John Seaman, 1.

Wiseman, Durbin and Hanna were duly elected trustees and Marquis, treasurer.

There was much interest and excitement manifested at this election and quite a number of the voters of the township responded. Aside from the local party designations of "Juntos" and "Brimstones" still prevailing to some extent at that day, and among whom the political contests were bitter and violent, there was a question of reform agitating the community in regard to the very loose and unsatisfactory manner in which the affairs of the school section had, in the long past, been managed.

Messrs. Wiseman, Hanna and Durbin were the reform candidates and succeeded by a small majority over the Old Fogies who, for several years, had had control of the rents, profits and issues of the section. The affairs of the section about this time being in a deplorable condition, called loudly for reform, and seemed to need the vigilance of some energetic men to unravel the tangled skein and bring order out of chaos. At that time all the fertile and productive section 16 in Malta township and in the close vicinity of the growing village of Malta would only bring into the treasury of the section for school purposes a small amount.

A few gallons of Moxahala whiskey, with hoop-poles, oak barb, and clapboards from the lease holders would suffice to pay the annual rent.

The lease holders seemed to command the situation and dictated to the trustees the amount of the yearly rents, when, where and in what manner it should be paid.

Annual rent was, therefore, at a very low rate, and to be paid when the several lessees pleased, and that in whiskey or in the product of the forest, or in corn at 25 cents per bushel, and that by the trustees exchanged for "store pay." Money seemed no longer legal tender with the lessees and trustees, when whiskey, oak bark, shingles, hoop-poles and corn could be substituted. The result of this kind of management produced nothing for the benefit of the common school fund and great wastes were being constantly committed upon the section by the recklessness of the lessees and the indifference of the trustees. This, however, was the case with nearly every section 16 in the county. So bad became the management that by the voice of the voters school sections everywhere in the county were ordered to be sold and the revenue derived therefrom has created a permanent fund, the proceeds of which will be a lasting benefit.

It will be observed by those acquainted with the names of the voters upon the list at that election, that death has been among them. Of the whole number only about ten are known to be living. Six only of the survivors now reside in the then township of Morgan.

It appears, then, that in a voting population of 66 persons after the lapse of 44 years, only ten of that number survive and only six of the survivors are residents of the township that then knew them.

Let those who may be inclined to examine into the vital statistics of the county reflect and speculate upon the probable duration of the lives of the men thus presented by the list of adults upon this poll book.

We notice among the ten surviving, the following are the only residents, namely: John E. Hanna, David Newman, Jacob Adams, Charles Robertson, R. E. Pinkerton and John B. Stone. The non-resident survivors are: John T. Arthur, W. C. Shugert, William Dawes and Edwin Corner.

In the spring of 1824 appeared at McConnelsville the first steamboat navigating the undisturbed waters of the Muskingum. The "Rufus Putnam," taking her name from one of the first pioneer settlers of Ohio, then a resident of Marietta, was the name of the first steamboat, a stranger in these waters and also to our people at that day an important event. The boat was built at Marietta, Capt. Green, Master, and James Leggett, then of Waterford, who died some years later in Windsor township, was the waterman who piloted the first steamer upon our river.

The "Rufus Putnam" unheralded made her appearance at our shore on a beautiful spring day in 1824. Our people being taken by surprise were on the alert and all excitement, noise and confusion, running to and fro, huzzahing, throwing up hats, and waving of handkerchiefs and other things not necessary to mention, prevailed, and nothing else being talked or thought of for some time afterwards, but the unexpected and unthought of appearance of the pioneer steamer.

She came up on a good spring freshet and continued on to Zanesville, bearing upon her pleasant decks and in beautiful weather a large and for that day a brilliant and gay party, comprising the elite, beauty and chivalry of the then antiquated village of Marietta.

At Zanesville her reception was in accordance with the times and the event. The officers, crew and passengers were sumptuously entertained by the hospitable and enterprising citizens of Zanesville and Putnam. Feasting, toasting, dancing, visiting and much noise was the order of the day while the boat remained.

On the return trip of the boat the whole people on both sides of the river, far interior, flocked to its banks to witness, to most of them, the first steamboat. She made the run from Zanesville to McConnelsville, on a big freshet, in something over an hour. In those days the loud sounding bell and steam horn were unknown and unused upon steamboats.

The arrival and departure of the boat were announced by the discharge of a small gun, let off upon her bow, the sound of which reverberated throughout valleys, hills and woods to a great distance.

The "Rufus Putnam" was of the high pressure kind, as nearly all steamers of that day were, and her puffing steam could be heard for miles. She neglected to throw out her lines at McConnelsville, both going up and coming down, because of the great crowd present, thereby disappointing and depriving our curious people from examining her inward workings and appointments, and depositing their dirt and tobacco juice upon her clean and well varnished decks and furniture.

After this adventure of the "Rufus Putnam," other steamers now and then passed up and down the river; but steamboating on the river did not become a permanent institution until after the completion of slack water navigation. Some few years intervened before the appearance to our people of another steamboat. The first follower of the "Rufus Putnam" was the "Speedwell," a slow, dirty, blackened and indifferent craft when compared with the fast, clean, bright and well appointed "Rufus Putnam." Her coming was announced to our people by a "solitary horseman, slowly wending his way" up the left bank of the Muskingum, who reported he had passed the unseemly craft at "Big Ludlow Ripple" an hour before her appearance at our landing.

Notwithstanding the indifferent appearance of this boat, our people hailed her with great joy, manifesting the same with frequent and loud noises by the use of a home-made swivel, and the frequent huzzas from the untamed throats of our men, women and children.

Since that day, steamboat navigation has made great rapidity in improvement and in no part of the world more striking than in the west and the southwest parts of our Union. Nine years only before the advent of the "Rufus Putnam" upon the Muskingum, the first steamboat trip was made from New Orleans to Louisville and Pittsburg, in May, 1815; the second and third trips in 1817. The application of steam to boats, cars, etc., has done more to people, to develop and build up the great west than any other means invented and introduced by man. In the early days of steamboating it required all the energies of Fitch, Rumsey, Evans, Fulton and others to bring the public to see their interests and to make this great invention completely triumphant over prejudice, ignorance and parsimony.

John Fitch was the first person who, under great difficulties, made application of steam to the propulsion of water-craft.

The following anecdote is related, representing Fitch's first trial in steamboating. At the time of making the exhibition, Fitch remarked to the scientific gentlemen who would condescend to witness it: "This, gentlemen, will be the mode of crossing the Atlantic in time, and although I may not live to see it, you may, when steam is preferred to all other modes of conveyance, and it will be particularly useful in ascending the Mississippi." He then retired, when a person present observed in a tone of deep sympathy: "Poor fellow, what a pity he is crazy."

A laughable and somewhat ludicrous scene took place in our village in the early days of the Democratic and Whig parties. One Isaac Pepper, a political adventurer, came to our village to establish and put in working order a Democratic Press. He met with ready encouragement and purchased from one of the partners of Wilkin & Christy his interest in the "Morgan Sentinel" newspaper, the first paper printed and published in the county.

The "Sentinel,' in its course, undertook to run in the neutral ruts, with a leaning towards Whiggery; pretending to neutrality, it scarcely pleased anyone. By such a course it became obnoxious with both parties and, consequently, suspended and shut up shop. Party spirit at this time was running high. The presidential contest between Clay and Jackson, Bank and Anti-Bank, were the engrossing political topics of the day, and politicians were greatly worked up and would fight one another "at the dropping of a hat."

In this memorable contest every man, besides a considerable sprinkling of women, and all the boys, arrayed themselves on one side or the other, and valiantly contended for what they conceived to be right.

On a certain day, Pepper repaired to the "Sentinel" office to take possession of the type, press and fixtures, and all the other things thereunto belonging. The Democrats and Whigs, lounging around, watching one another, noticing the movements of the valiant Pepper, made a rush pell mell into the office, the one party (Whigs) demanding an equal division of the type, etc., the other (Democrats) objecting and claiming all. On the run of the fighting politicians towards the office, which was a small frame building upon the Mrs. Powell lot, coats were thrown, sleeves were rolled up, arms—offensive and defensive—seized, and a war of demolition threatened by the parties against the press, if they failed to accomplish their ends and demands. The combatants quarreled and swore terribly and severely impeached each others' characters. At length an ardent Whig, who saw Pepper was likely to take the press, type and all the fixtures to himself, by the aid of law and force, and start a Jackson paper in their midst, proposed to compromise the difficulty, that is to give and take a little. He suggested that a mixed paper representing both parties, should be published. On one side of the sheet the cause of Whiggery, Clay and the United States Bank should be advocated, while on the other side, Democracy, Jackson and Anti-Bank should be sustained and have a hearing. A no less ardent Democrat present protested and remarked that "A paper of that kind, sent out among the people, would be a d——d pretty looking thing, with Democratic truth on one side and then, to turn it over, to find on the other, nothing but d——d Whig lies; they would have nothing of it." This last sockdollager, coming up so opportunely, settled the "Press War" and Pepper bore off the spoils.

In the melee, the same ardent Whig got hold of a large spread eagle type and was about to make away with it, when discovered by a Democrat, he was commanded to lay it down, that "the British Lion would be more appropriate and suit him and his principles much better."

Pepper started his paper, ardently advocated the claims of Andrew Jackson resulting in a majority in the county of about 200. Then it was that the Whigs not to be outdone and baffled in this way, forthwith started up a new press, and then it was war to the knife and knife to the hilt, with occasional knock downs, some biting, gouging and scratching among the valiant politicians of 1832.

In 1822 it was, that Adams and Shugert bought the first drove of hogs in the county. They were gathered previous to their movement to eastern market, upon the farm of Amasa Hoyt, in Center township, now owned and occupied by Mr. David Drake. At the time and place of gathering these hogs an altercation took place between William C. Johnson, a hired hand of Adams and Shugert, and William Murray, a farmer of Meigsville township, who was there with hogs to sell and deliver, which affray resulted in the killing of Mr. Murray by a pocketknife in the hands of Johnson.

Johnson attempted his escape, but was arrested a few miles distant from the scene of the murder, was tried by the court in McConnelsville at the May term in 1823, found guilty of murder in the second degree and sent to the Ohio penitentiary for life, and after service of about twenty years, was pardoned by the then governor. The killing took place in the field east of Drake's present residence. The old farm house, then occupied by Hoyt, stood across the road about opposite to the place of the murder. The jury who tried the case were William Silvey, Jeremiah Conaway, James Frisby, Jacob R. Price, Jonathan Porter, John Hughes, James A. Gillespie, Lyman Lawrence, John P. Anderson, William Montgomery, Thomas Campbell and John W. Johnson.

They are all deceased. This was the first known murder case in the county. We have had other murders since that time, but no executions have ever taken place.

Hogs then brought from $1.50 to $2.00 per hundred. At that day the woods afforded abundance of beech, oak and hickory mast upon which the hogs fed and were chiefly fattened; the farmers, by feeding them an allowance of corn for a short time, made them suitable for market. Adams and Shugert, after collecting their hogs, went with them to Marietta, there crossed the Ohio, thence to Clarksburg, now in West Virgina, thence to Winchester, Va., and thence to Washington City, where they found a market. They were 50 days upon the road. The hands were paid only 50c a day, and two meals. At this early day there was no other product of the county but the hogs that brought any considerable amount of money to the producer.

Other agricultural products, such as cattle, horses and sheep, could not well be spared, nor could they find a ready market at any price. If there was any surplus, it was disposed of to the newcomers who, for a time after their settlement, were consumers until they became producers.

The money thus obtained by the sale of hogs enabled a goodly number of the pioneer settlers to pay for their lands which at that day they had entered from the government at $2 per acre, payable in installments.

This business of buying and driving hogs was continued by Adams & Shugert for some three or four years, and was the only source our poor farmers had of obtaining money, which was then very scarce, to pay out their lands and meet their payments of taxes.

The contrast of that period with the present, in commerce and transportation, shows even our people here in Morgan, a vast increase and improvement. Then fifty years ago, to take a bunch of hogs to the Baltimore or Washington market, the drove was 50 days on the road. Now, fifty hours will put the hogs into the same market, half or more of that time will be taken getting the hogs from McConnelsville to a suitable railroad depot or station.

John B. Stone, Esq., of McConnelsville, has handed me the following abstract, in the handwriting of Timothy Gaylord, deceased, showing the result of the presidential election in Morgan county in the year 1828.

The abstract presents the full vote received by each candidate in the several townships of the county. This statement should be thus preserved, for it may be presumed that, in after years, not a vestige of the vote will be found except, perhaps, among the musty or neglected files of the secretary of state's office at Columbus. No official count of the vote for president is kept at the county seat. The poll books of such elections are carried by the sheriff to Columbus and there opened and, after a time, disposed of as waste paper.

Abstract of Votes Given in Morgan County, for President, in 1828, Namely:

Twps.	Jackson	Adams	Majorities	
Morgan	69	123	00	54
Manchester	80	30	50	00
Deerfield	44	59	00	15
Windsor	43	44	00	1
York	57	41	16	00
Penn	31	56	00	25
Olive Green	48	12	36	00
Meigsville	47	39	8	00
Bristol	72	57	15	00
Noble	66	20	46	00
Union	42	16	26	00
Brookfield	58	44	14	00
Olive	80	60	20	00
Bloom	61	59	2	00
Center	43	37	6	00
Total	841	697	239	95

It will be observed that the Morgan county of 1828 is not the Morgan county of 1873. Since that day the whole of the townships of Olive Green, Noble, Brookfield and Olive, and half of Manchester have been lost to Morgan county and incorporated in the new county of Noble. This territory gave Jackson 166 majortiy over Adams. To overcome this majority, which was the firm, steadfast and reliable majority of the Democrats of the county, the anti-Democratic politicians got the legislature, in 1845, to annex to Morgan from Athens county the two townships of Marion and Homer. Yet this annexation proved a failure in producing the expected political change. The prospect for creating the new county of Noble was gotten up and, in 1851, passed through the legislature, by which suicidal scheme Morgan county was despoiled of her best territory.

While this despoiling scheme was going on, and being agitated from center to circumference, the Whig party put up David Ball of Malta township, as a candidate for representative. The new county party in the east end, who still voted in Morgan county, anxious for their new county, interrogated Ball to know how he stood on the county question. Ball answered in the following terse, Quakerish and satisfactory manner:

Malta, Ohio,_____, 1848.

Friend McGarry:—

I am with thee in all thy new county projects.

I am thine affectionately,
DAVID BALL.

This epistle was a comforter to the New County party. Because of this letter, Ball was elected, and Noble county, to the disappointment and chagrin of everyone opposed to the disintegration of the county, was afterwards, in 1851, created and became a fixed fact.

Other interesting facts can be gathered from this abstract. Deerfield township, then anti-Democratic, has since become strongly Democratic; Windsor, then very close, is still the same way; York has largely increased her Democratic majority; Penn has increased her anti-Democratic vote, while the Democratic vote has in no wise improved; Meigsville, then Democratic, still adheres to her ancient faith; Bristol is much larger Democratic than at that period; Union, then strongly Democratic, has greatly backslidden; Bloom township, in those days as now, very close; Center has greatly improved her Democratic vote in the last 45 years; Manchester, then a full township, with only half now in Morgan, gives her old Democratic majority; Morgan township, including Malta, then "National Republican" by a large majority, has been anti-Democratic ever since, keeping up with the alteration of things and the change of names.

In the settlement of Morgan county, and, in fact, all over Ohio, the people for many years were sorely pressed for the article of good and cheap salt. This article of primary importance could not be well dispensed with among the white inhabitants, nor were they able to find a substitute. In this particular the Indian, unlike the white man, can live and enjoy good health without it. The Indian subsists almost entirely upon meat and can well preserve it for his immediate needs, by "jerking" or drying it over a slow fire. Salt, therefore, with the white man being an article of absolute necessity, he was obliged to bring it across the Allegheney mountains on pack horses for many years after the first settlement of the country, at an expense of six or eight dollars per bushel. This exorbitant price for salt continued to exist until the discovery of salt water of a strong character was made by boring down deep into the hard rocks.

This discovery made salt much more plenty and brought down the price, to the great joy of the old pioneers everywhere west of the mountains.

It was truly a great discovery and advantageous to our people, for it was supposed that the west would always be dependent on the Atlantic coast for salt, and deeply deplored as a serious drawback on the prosperity of this beautiful region.

Springs of salt-water might be found all over southern Ohio and were so highly prized that the government reserved from the sale surveys in which they were located. Yet they were of so poor and weak a quality as to require several hundred gallons of water to make a bushel of salt, and that a very inferior article. Notwithstanding its inferiority, compared with that brought over the mountains, it could be used, and our pioneers thereby saved money, at that day not very plentiful in their purses.

Some time about 1817, Nathaniel or Moses Ayers, of Muskingum county, then quite a young man, left his home and went to the "Kanawha Salt Works," then a place of considerable resort for laborers, fortune seekers and unpunished criminals. He remained there some time, engaged at the works, learning the arts and mysteries connected with the boring of wells and the manufacturing of salt, as then carried on in that region. With this knowledge thus obtained, he returned home and put down a well and made the first salt upon the Muskingum river.

This first well was sunk above Duncan Falls, on the right bank of the Muskingum. From this first enterprise of Mr. Ayers' sprung into existence the numerous salt furnaces now dotting the banks of the Muskingum from Hooksburg, in Morgan county, to the corporation line of Zanesville city. A few years after the Ayers experiment the late Zurial Sherwood sunk a well upon the farm in Malta Twp. now owned by James Moore (Walker, Jenkins farms).

This was the first, and for many years the only, salt well in the county of Morgan, affording practical relief to our people, both in the price and quality of salt. After the success of Mr. Sherwood, there sprung into existence some 25 or more other salt wells and furnaces on both sides of the river, commencing at the county line and extending as far down as the mouth of Turkey Run in Windsor township.

About 15 of the furnaces are in full blast at this time, affording all the salt necessary for home consumption, besides a large quantity for other markets, amounting to at least $80,000 per annum.

Writing about salt and salt springs, I conceive it would not be out of place to here relate an incident that took place at one of these salt springs at an early day. I am indebted to the late Dr. Hildreth of Marietta for the principal of the matter related:

Old Silverheels

The best of these salt springs were resorted to at a very early day by the settlers, who generally assembled in gangs of six or eight persons with the necessary vessels to boil in, with their pack horses and provisions, camped out for some days in the vicinity of the spring, and there manufactured their salt. One of the most noted of these springs was upon Salt Creek, near what is now called Chandlersville in Muskingum county.

A few years after the closing of the long and bloody Indian War, in 1795, a party of white men from the Olive Green settlement repaired to this spring for the purpose of making salt. While engaged in this business a noted Indian, well known to the pioneers in early days by the name of "Silverheels," was hunting near the above spring, and called at the camp. In times of peace, the intercourse of the Indians with the whites was friendly, with perfect confidence and unrestrained. Old "Silverheels" had lived, and perhaps at that time his wigwam was at or near the mouth of Bald Eagle Creek in Windsor township, in this county, and near a ripple in the Muskingum river, well known to all navigators of the river by the name of "Silverheels" and which name it retained until obliterated and lost by slackwater navigation.

The party of salt makers had with them an ample supply of the favorite beverage of the day and, knowing the Indian very much relished whiskey, offered it to him in frequent and liberal potations. After taking a few drinks, the spirit of the old warrior was aroused and, as is their custom, he related his war exploits; that in his various battles and marauding excursions he had taken the scalps of 16 whites. Amongst others, during the late Indian war, he stated he had taken the scalp of an old man a little below the mouth of Olive Green Creek on the Muskingum river, not farm from the Block House, which was then located above where

Beverly now stands. Old "Silverheels" minutely described this scalp as having two crowns on the top of the head and that he carefully cut and divided it so as to present two scalps, and sold them to the British at Detroit for $50 each. From "Silverheels'" narrative, it appears that the old man at the time he shot him, was gathering May apples, and had the bosom of his hunting shirt full of them. He minutely described the old man's musket, with its iron bands around it; but being in haste at the time, looking for pursuit from the Block House, and the gun being of no use to him, he had hidden it in the hollow of a tree a short distance up the river.

The salt makers took particular interest in this portion of "Silverheels'" feats, as several of them were acquainted with Abel Sherman and, at the time, lived with him in the Block House, and all were familiar with the fact of his being killed by the Indians in the manner and at the place described by the old warrior. As it happened, one of Mr. Sherman's sons was of that salt making party, and to be sure of the truth of old "Silverheels'" statement, he returned directly home.

He made search and found, in the rotten wood and earth of the decayed tree, an old musket. The stock was much wasted and the barrel quite rusty, but sufficient remained to identify it as the gun of his father, thus proving the truth of the old Indian's statement that he was personally concerned in the death of Abel Sherman. A short time after this, the dead body of old "Silverheels" was found by a hunter, lying in the ashes of his camp-fire, pierced with a rifle bullet. Old "Silverheels" was of the Shawnee tribe, which tribe from time immemorial occupied the valley of the Muskingum as their hunting grounds, sharing it with the Wyandots, the Mingoes, and other tribes when on friendly terms and not engaged in war with each other. After the war, old "Silverheels" seems to have isolated himself from his tribe and, being a great and successful hunter, pitched his tent in the midst of abundant game and fish, dwelling in the close vicinity of the mouth of Bald Eagle Creek, on the right bank of the Muskingum, and near to the formerly well known ripple, named by the early settlers, "Silverheels." There he lived and there he met death by the bullet from the unerring rifle in the hands of the practiced white man, the natural foe of the treacherous red man.

The Militia

It may be said that in 1820 the militia of Morgan county was first completely organized, consisting of the 1st regiment, — brigade, — division of the Ohio State Militia.

Alexander McConnell was the colonel who in time became major general; B. W. Talbott, lieutenant colonel who afterwards became colonel of the regiment; and Asa Emerson, major, who unfortunately failed in his promotion because of an extraordinary feat of horsemanship performed on the parade ground on the occasion of the first general muster. The major in person was long, lean and lank, standing over six feet in his stockings, dressed in gaudy, but not expensive or fine regimentals; spurs on his heels with several in his head; mounted upon a rather diminutive, untrimmed but spirited young charger, made his first appearance upon the field, in company with the other regimental and staff officers, all bedecked and bedazzled, and brilliantly dressed, with nodding plumes, pendant from three-cornered chapeaus.

The martial music of that day was discordant, and the major's horse having no ear for such music, took fright at the thumping drum and shrill-sounding fife, and started full tilt, first down along the front of the regiment, then turned the left flank and made a like exhibition of himself along the rear and then from the front charged and broke the center, dispersing and routing whole companies as though an hostile foe had appeared among them. The spurs on his heels dug deep into the flanks, sides and belly of the frightened beast; the shouts from a thousand throats, the unceasing music of a dozen drums, and the loud, thundering shots from old war blunderbusses added much to the speed, prolongation and perils of the major's ride. He finally brought himself and horse up in a fence corner, where he dismounted, much discomfited and badly demoralized. This was the first and last appearance of the major upon the ensanguined (equine blood only) field of Mars. He soon after retired from military life, disgusted with its tactics, discipline and rules of promotion, and many years ago died at his home near Luke Chute in Windsor township. And with a quartermaster, paymaster, adjutant, sergeant-major, drum-major, fife-major, and chaplain, appointments made by the colonel, the regiment was prepared for duty and service.

The regiment was about 500 strong and first mustered upon the farm of Joseph Devereaux, located on Mann's Fork in Bristol Twp., now owned and occupied by Rufus Cotton. The regiment appeared upon parade fully armed and equipped, some with and many without guns; some with walking sticks, others with corn stalks, and because of the latter being the prevailing arm of defense at these musters, they were everywhere known and called the "Cornstalk Militia."

At this general muster, being a new featured public affair, and our people being then of a more social nature than now, full of fun and frolic, came in from 15 miles around about, men, women and children, to participate in and witness the performances of the day.

Whiskey, cider, apples and gingerbread prevailed and was copiously taken to appease thirst and hunger of "man's innards." In those days, it was fashionable to thus indulge and, therefore, universally tolerated, to the extent of each individual's taste and inclination. Strong drink such as whiskey, it being the prevailing beverage, was considered as much of an article of necessity for the support of man, and especially those any way exposed to the vicissitudes of the weather or engaged in any laborious employment, as meat or bread.

Temperance societies were then unknown hereabouts, and a person who did not offer his neighbor or friend a dram, even when calling at his house, was thought a stingy fellow, and as much despised as if he should fail to observe other more necessary acts of hospitality.

The law of the present day, however, regulates such acts of hospitality, and visits the offender in certain cases with severe pains and penalties.

Then prohibition with its new light was unknown and unsung. On such occasions, fights of "fist and skull" were common. The combatants purposely met at such gatherings to settle in that way any differences or unpleasantnesses that might in the past have been brewing or existing among them.

General musters at that day were important institutions, now unknown, unwept, unhonored and unsung. They are of the past, the like of which we shall never again look upon.

At this first general muster first appeared the Olive Green Independent Rifles Company, John Whitmore, captain. They were the observed of all observers, 100 strong, composed of the bone and sinew of the townships of Olive Green, Olive, and Center, large, resolute and fierce-looking fellows. Their uniforms were cheap, entirely home made, consisting of a linsey woolsey, deep blue hunting shirt, fringed with red, butternut linsey pants, and every man armed with a squirrel rifle of that day which, in the hands of these stalwart men and defenders of our country's rights, would bring down the game or foe at every shot. The officers wore the same kind of uniforms as the privates, with some outlandish insignia to distinguish them from the common soldier. They would march and counter march, adroitly go through the rifle manual and perform all the military evolutions common at that day, and by way of variety, a little of the maneuvers and drill of the Indian, making themselves the applause of the gaping audience.

Captain Whitmore was the center of attraction, a hale fellow well met; one of the first settlers in the county; an expert woodsman and hunter and one of the successors to the Indians in their bountiful hunting grounds upon the waters of Duck and Olive Green Creeks; a crack shot, the eye his mark. He was intelligent and communicative and, in backwoods adventures, trials, exploits and hair-breadth escapes, of which he was a part, in their relation he was interesting.

Old hunters, like old sailors, sometimes indulge themselves in "yarning it." Captain Whitmore used to tell about himself the following remarkable hunting story:

One winter day more than half a century ago, he relates, he went out from his cabin to hunt deer. Unfortunately for successful hunting, it had snowed and become frozen, forming a crust which, when walked upon, made a noise, startling to the keen hearing of the timid deer. In his hunt it was not long before he came in sight of four deer, one old buck and three does. The noise upon the frozen crust started them off at full speed; the captain followed, came in sight; again they fled; again he followed, and so on until a late hour in the afternoon, the captain, over hill and dale pursued the fast retreating game. This part of the captain's story seemed natural enough; but the way in which the hunt terminated somewhat staggered the credulity of his listeners.

The last stop the deer made was down in a deep hollow with sloping hills on all sides. The captain had followed the deer all day without a shot, and he was one of that kind of men who delighted in the pursuit, but felt much better when in possession of the object. He relates that he cautiously approached the brow of the hill, and discovered his game contentedly browsing, several hundred yards distant and too far off to bring them down with his gun. To bag his game he relates that he resorted to the following **stratagem**: With his practiced eye he measured the distance and took close observations of the surroundings. He resolved to have his deer, and this being his last and only chance, as the sun was then just peeping above the western horizon, he prepared himself for the contest.

He wore a roomy, long, Virginia hunting shirt, very common in those days, now scarcely to be seen; under this shirt he carefully placed his gun next to his body, and for safety and security, the muzzle past his head and against one of his shoulders; he then closely wrapped and belted the shirt around his body and his gun, laid himself horizontally upon the snow and commenced to roll down hill towards the deer, all the time keeping an eye out as to the course and distance and obstructions. The deer seeing the object coming towards them, moved not. They seemed to wonder at such unusual movement, and were dumb to all danger. Before starting on his rolling trip, the captain had selected his tree, about, as he judged, one hundred yards from the deer and in the direct line of his approach. In his rolling process coming to his tree, he got up and took position behind it, selecting the old buck, and brought him down dead in the midst of the flock.

The captain was then satisfied that the deer in due time would all be his; for the deer, under such a state of affairs, will stand in seeming wonder and astonishment at the picture presented, and by the rifle of the skilled hunter, is made a certain and easy prey. The captain continued to stand behind the tree, and as fast as he could load and shoot, a deer fell, until four of them lay weltering in their blood. He dressed and hung up his game, and hastened to his home some miles distant, returning early next morning with a team and bob-sled and brought in the spoils of his great chase; after which there was much feasting with the captain and his neighbors.

Scarcity of Small Change

In those early days, of which I have been writing about, our people were put to much inconvenience in regard to small change in ordinary business transactions. Our change then consisted of 6¼ cents (fips), 12½ cents (bits or levies), 25 cents Spanish quarters, and 50 cents — generally United States half dollars. The dime and half-dime, so prevalent among us before the Rebellion, at that time had no existence. There are boys, young men I may say, upon our streets, jumping about stores, banks and business places, who cannot at first sight tell the value of any of these coins.

They are banished and out of circulation, and consequently unknown to the rising generation of modern financiers. This is the result of an exclusive paper money circulation, which we have now, save and except the base nickel which freely circulates, stamped with the legend, "In God We Trust."

Those so anxious for the recognition of God in the constitution may, for the present, be consoled by looking upon this legend and, besides, may receive much encouragement.

It is a truth in financial matters that gold and silver will not circulate with depreciated paper money. The former is hoarded and kept back, or made an article of commerce and trade, while the latter is used for exclusive circulation.

These young chaps, however, can tell you all about the value of a "Shinplaster," with their eyes shut, or by the sense of feeling or smelling. To remedy this great scarcity in the matter of change, in an early day our people were compelled to resort to the use of what was then called "Cut Money." The "Cut Money" manufacturer not only cut money, but he made money without permit or authority from sovereignty. He ran his big or little machine with impunity—no one to molest or hinder or make him afraid.

Any and everybody could, and many of them did, manufacture cut money if they should happen to have the material at hand and there was a necessity. The process of fixing up cut money was more simple and more easily accomplished than in the process of manufacturing "Shinplasters" nowadays. The manufacturer would apply his cutting instrument to the silver half dollar, and out of it would drop five "Sharpshins," as they were called—that is, out of 50 cents he made five 12½-cent pieces, or 62½ cents. Out of a quarter of a dollar, he made five fippenny-bits or 31¼ cents.

Our people received this kind of change in all their small business, and those who resorted to the manufacturing of such change, made it pay. It became such an evil, however, that the legislature had to interfere to put a stop to it by enactments. The "Cut Money" was finally gathered up and sent to the United States mint, and then, by congressional enactments followed by liberal coinage of dimes and half-dimes, quarters and halves.

With this "Cut Money" our people were in some places annoyed with the issue of individual "Shinplasters." The shinplasters passed current if the individual or firm issuing them could have a credit in the neighborhood; if not, but should be suspected, like a bank, of being insolvent or about to break, "a run upon them" was sometimes made quite exciting among holders and annoying to the "shinplaster" factors. It was a common thing to counterfeit these shinplasters, but it is not remembered that any prosecutions or convictions were ever had against the offenders.

The opinion of the lawyers at that day was that as the currency was illegal and without authority, counterfeiting the same could not, under the circumstances, be maintained and punished; but forging the name of the individual or firm, might. Finally, want of confidence, counterfeiting and the repelling appearance of the filthy rags, drove them out of circulation.

What is to be lamented at this day is that no one ever sees or handles, as a medium of exchange, the old-fashioned dime, half-dime, fip, bit, quarter, half-pistereen, etc., once so handy, convenient and safe. The government at Washington has taken up the shinplaster business, banishing coin, and undertakes to furnish a substitute representing the sovereignty of the state, in the shape of pictured and printed pieces of paper, making them a legal tender.

In an early day, the natural productions of the Muskingum river were immense. Before the banks were deprived of timber, which grew in quantity and to a great size, and its bed much more contracted than at present, and before the erection of the state dams, it was plentifully stored with fish. The black cat and the pike were the largest among the races of its finny tribe. The yellow cat, white perch, spotted or green perch (called by fishermen nowadays green bass), salmon, sturgeon, buffalo, white and red tail suckers are all fine fish, weighing from five to 50 pounds. The sturgeon fish, which was once so plentiful, has become extinct and is no longer found in our waters. But in its stead we have what the fishermen call the lake bass passing into our river since the construction of the Ohio canal. One of our ferrymen, years ago, being withal an observant man, one from whom information might be obtained and somewhat of a fisherman, used to relate to the loungers who frequented the ferry landing that he at times had observed a black mudcat in the river here at this place that was enormous and its weight he could not guess but that it was at least two feet between the eyes and it had on one or two occasions obstructed the progress of the ferry boat so that he was compelled to back off and propel around the obstacle. The relator of this fish story was not that other old ferryman who, when asked by an inquisitive stranger how long he had lived hereabout, replied: "Stranger, do you see them hills over there?" pointing to the Malta hills. "I was here before they were, and always enjoyed good health." At this the stranger, who had become an annoyance to the old fisherman, subsided, paid his toll and departed. If not a wiser man, he was certainly a badly bluffed individual, and so left.

The black catfish weighs as high as 100 pounds; but that size is generally taken in the Ohio, and towards the mouth of the Muskingum. When fat, they make fine eating, especially if light salted and dried. The pike is the king of fish in the western waters. It is related that in 1788 a pike was taken in the Muskingum river, by Judge Gilbert Devoll, weighing 100 pounds. The judge was a tall man, but when the fish was suspended on a pole, from his shoulder, its tail dragged on the ground, so that it was about six feet in length.

About 80 years ago in the primitive days of fishing here upon the Muskingum river, when the Indian seemed to be master of the situation when all along the banks of the Muskingum the forest was dense, with the long tree-arms almost interlocking each other from the right and left banks with here and there a cleared patch with the hunter's and fisherman's hut hid in the thicket, a professional fisherman, daring and always successful, by the name of Jim Patterson, went forth, as was his habit and as his wants required, to take a few pounds of fish: "I didn't want much nor I wasn't looking for much," anchored his canoe out in the still waters of the river just at dark, threw out his lines and, wrapping himself in his blanket, lay down in his boat for a nap. A black catfish came along and seized his hook. This fish was so large and possessed such strength as to drag the canoe and light anchor stone from its moorings, far down the river in deep water, where Patterson found himself on waking, on the head of a small island with canoe, fish and all things safe. The fish weighed 96 pounds.

In early days the most of the fish were taken on the trot line. Our early and most celebrated and successful fishermen here upon the Muskingum and in this neighborhood were Hand and Craft. They fished together and seemed always to be in such good luck, and catching them in great numbers where others would fail. They would catch in a night half a barrel or more upon their lines. They fished altogether with the hook and spear. They resided upon the river in Windsor township and immigrated hence to the west, some years since, as their occupation was gone when the waters of the clear and beautiful Muskingum became muddy and obstructed by dams and violently disturbed by the paddles of the steamer. To the early settlers, on the borders of our river, and even upon creeks, the fish taken furnished no small part of their animal food, especially in the spring and fall seasons. In the spring the fish were taken on hooks, but in the fall, after frost, when the water was low and clear, they were taken by torchlight with the spear or three-pronged gig.

The mode of taking fish with the gig was about thus: A large torch, made from light wood splinters, was held up in the bow of the canoe, for that was our only small craft in use in early days, to attract the attention of the fish and give light to the spearman. The canoe was guided by the man in the stern, giving it motion and direction with a paddle. A skillful spearman, all things in working order, would often load a canoe during one evening's hunt. The light of the torch attracts the fish, and it seems to be amazed, and will seldom try to escape, while by daylight, scarcly a fish can be seen by this mode. There is at this day a noticeable falling off, both in quantity and quality, of fish, when compared with the period of 50 or 70 years ago; and all the laws passed by our legislatures for the protection and preservation of fish seem to have thus far failed to produce what is so much desired. The Indians had a mode of taking the pike fish which is still, to some extent, practiced by the white man. A fish weighing a pound or more is fastened to a strong hook and line, by forcing it through the length of the body to near the tail. This is thrown out into the stream where the pike are believed to congregate and where it is in the habit of lying in wait for its prey, and then drawn rapidly into shore, so as to make the bait jump along on the surface, imitating a fish pursued by another; the pike, if in sight, instantly seizes upon the fish and is sure to be hooked.

The salmon may be taken in the same way. Hand and Craft, the celebrated fishermen spoken of above, were quite successful in taking both pike and salmon by this method learned from the Indians.

Wild Game

I have been reminded by an old citizen of the large flocks of wild pigeons that flew over our village in 1819. The heavens for many days were fairly dark with these birds, in their passage in the morning from the west and in the evenings in their going back. They could be heard flying early in the morning and late in the night. Since that period, we have witnessed similar and partial flights of these birds, but nothing to equal that of 1819. Their evening passage was from their feeding grounds in the east and south to their roosts far off in the west. They are a bird of rapid flight; no other can equal them. They have been taken at their roosts here in the western country with fresh and undigested South Carolina rice in their craws; showing that they fly long distances and with great rapidity. Hunters with torches and poles visit their roosts and slay thousands of them.

In this neighborhood they were taken on the wing, the hunter placing himself on the highest hill in the vicinity, where the flight of the birds was necessarily low.

This great pigeon flight in the early history of the country reminds me of an unprecedented migration or traveling of gray squirrels. About this period, when the sky was obscured by the flight of wild pigeons, the Muskingum river was literally covered with squirrels, swimming across it from the east to the west. This particular migration of the squirrels was remarkable and their number immense. In their course they leaped and swam over every obstacle and stream in their way.

There was no stopping them in their appointed course, except the club in the hands of men and boys, who would meet them in the stream and slay them by tens, hundreds and thousands, making them into pot-pies, fries, stews, etc., and upon which our pioneer people fared sumptuously for many days. Equal and perhaps more savory were these dishes to the appetites of our people here in the wilderness of the Muskingum, than were the quail and manna bestowed upon Moses and his party of Israelites in the wilderness of Egypt.

The course of this migratory movement of this interesting quadruped was never satisfactroily explained or accounted for, except it was in the search of food, and that cause is generally accepted as a full solution of the phenomenon, because it appears the most reasonable; yet the fact was, they left behind them an apparent abundance to enter a field of apparent scarcity; but the squirrel knew his wants and by instinct he was directed.

There has been no such migration of the squirrel taken place since the period of time above mentioned. Previous to 1819, it is related that the gray squirrel, in the fall of certain years, became itinerant, traveling simultaneously in millions from the north to the south, destroying whole fields of corn in a few days, if not immediately gathered, and eating everything in their way, like African locusts or the modern "Colorado Potato Bug," while they traveled forward without stopping long in any place, swimming large rivers and, perhaps, before winter returning again by the same route towards the north.

Of the period we write about, 1819, and prior thereto, wild game, such as deer and turkeys, was plentiful in the vicinity of our village. Turkeys in large flocks and deer in droves of ten to twenty were common in certain seasons of the year.

Venison and turkey were favorite and common dishes and hugely enjoyed by our early villagers. The Wards, Priests, and other hunters from Wolf and Sunday Creeks in a later day kept our people in bountiful supply of these desirable meats, so that in the greater part of the year every cabin-joist was kept well hung and burdened with large, fat and juicy saddles of venison. In the fall of the year the beech mast abounded in the woods along the river and creek bottoms, which brot in the turkeys in large flocks.

The wild turkey would sometimes depredate upon the cornfields and grain stacks, compelling the inhabitants to gather their corn early and to cover their stacks of grain with brush. Great numbers were killed with the rifle, caught in pens, killed with clubs and dogs. The wild turkey and the deer have disappeared from our woods and, perhaps, not one can at this time be found within the bounds of the county. About this period we could hear something about bears and panthers. They were at one time in the remembrance of the white man, common; they were not, however, nearly so numerous or daring as the wolf and wild-cat.

All these beasts of the forests were fond of hogs and pigs and were, at times, quite annoying to the early settler, but the bear and the panther were more shy and but seldom repeated their visits with that boldness of the wolf and wild-cat among the sheep and hogs.

The manner of taking the wild turkey in pens was to build an enclosure out of fence rails or poles, about two feet high, covered close and well secured with like material. A trench was dug about a foot or 18 inches deep, commencing on the outside of the pen and terminating about the center, both ends being graded. Corn was then strewn for some distance to the right, left and in front, at the entrance along the ditch, and throughout the pen.

The turkeys, coming in flocks, would follow up the corn trail, and in a few minutes the pen would be full of game. After eating the corn, the turkey would attempt to escape its prison, but invariably failed, it being the nature of the bird, except when feeding, to elevate its head and look for a place of escape at the top, not for one moment looking downward at the place of its entrance. Thus by this mode large numbers were taken in and about the cornfields in the early settlement of the country and our village.

A full grown wild turkey would weigh from sixteen to thirty pounds, and was very fat. They were, therefore, by no means an "unhandy bird." One of them would suffice a large family at a meal, with several platefulls left. No complaint as "too little for one and not enough for two," like that of the old elder of the ministry, was ever heard from our people in those good old days.

Windsor Township

Windsor is the oldest settled township in the county. It came into Morgan from Washington county in the organization of the former. It lies entirely within what is called the "Ohio Company's Purchase."

In brief, the "Ohio Company" was an association of persons who purchased from the "Continental Congress," in 1787, then sitting in New York City, one and a half millions of acres in the "Great Western Territory of the Union," and contracted to pay therefor sixty-six and two-thirds cents per acre. From failure of some of the associates to pay for their shares and other causes, the company became possessed of only 964,285 acres.

This tract was located on the Ohio and Muskingum rivers, which was then represented to be the best part of the whole western country.

A better and more thorough knowledge of the geography of the Great West proves the representations of the explorer to have been somewhat erroneous.

From the first settlement of the purchasers in April, 1788, to Wayne's battle and peace with the Indians in 1793, the settlers were constantly in danger from their savage foes. Notwithstanding the almost constant danger existing for five or more years, to the settlers, the country was gradually filling up and locations were being made at various desirable and attractive points.

The immigration, during these troublous times, could not confine itself to Marietta and vicinity, it branched out into the wilderness, forming into companies or squads, erected buildings from the huge trees of the forest for the defense and convenience of the inhabitants, and commenced upon the improvement of their claims, looking towards and depending upon Marietta for a portion of their indispensable supplies and aid in case of urgent necessity or a place of retreat when inevitable.

In the fall of 1790 a colony of 36 men began a settlement at an advanced position upon the left bank of the Muskingum, at a location called Big Bottom. It was called Big

Bottom, and still retains the name, from its size, being four or five miles in length and from a half to three-quarters of a mile wide, and containing more fine land than any other point upon the river below Zanesville.

For the following material facts in connection with the Indian massacre at Big Bottom I am, to some extent, indebted to the pages of "Pioneer History," by Dr. Hildreth, in 1848, a book out of print and perhaps little consulted by the present generation of dashing, moving, restless and money-making Americans.

These settlers erected a large block-house on the first or lower bottom and a few rods from the river. They were chiefly young, unmarried men, and but little acquainted with Indian warfare or military rule. This temporary and unfinished fortification stood on the farm now owned and occupied by Obediah Brokaw, and about a mile above the Roxbury landing.

The block-house, which might accommodate all of them in an emergency, was built of large beech logs, procured in the immediate vicinity, rather open and not well filled in between. The finishing job was put off for a more convenient season. The home was unenclosed with pickets and other outside defenses. The inmates became careless and indifferent, neglecting to adopt any regular system of defense and omitted to place guards regularly at the several approaches. Being without order and discipline, they left their guns standing in different corners of the house. About 20 men usually slept and stayed in the building, a part of whom were absent at the time of the attack.

The weather for some time previous to the attack had been cold, and the Muskingum was frozen so as to be passable upon the ice. On Sunday, January 2nd, 1791, there was a thaw, with the ground partially covered with snow.

It was not customary, in the depth of winter, for the Indians to go out on war parties, and these settlers thought themselves safe from their depredations during the long winter months.

Francis and Isaac Choate, members of the colony, had erected their cabin and commenced clearing their lots, about 20 rods above the block-house and a little back from the river. Thomas Shaw and James Patton lived with them. About the same distance below the garrison was an old clearing and a small cabin made several years before, under the laws of Virginia, which Asa or Eleazer Bullard had fitted up and then occupied. The Indians' warpath from their Sandusky towns to the mouth of the Muskingum passed along on top of the opposite high ridge and in sight of the river.

During the last summer the Indians had been hunting and loitering about the settlements at Waterford and Wolf Creek mills, and became well acquainted with the situation of things and the manner in which the whites lived; thus pretending friendship, some of the settlers, not apprehending danger, had carelessly occupied their own cabins. With this knowledge thus obtained, the Indians planned and fitted out a war party for destruction of the Waterford settlement, which was in and about where Beverly is now located. When the Indians started out on this expedition against Waterford, they were not aware of there being a station at Big Bottom until they came in sight of it from their war path upon the high ground on the west side of the river in the afternoon of January 2, 1791. From this lookout upon the ridge they had a complete view of all that part of the bottom below them, and could well see how the men were occupied and the defenseless condition of the fortifications. The Indians, after holding council as to the mode of attack, crossed the river on the ice, a little above the block-house, and divided their party into two attacking divisions; the larger one was to assault the block-house and the other was to make prisoners of those in the outside cabins, causing no alarm to those in the main building.

The plan was skillfully made and promptly carried out. Cautiously approaching the upper cabin, they found the inmates at supper. A portion of the Indian party entered the door while others stood without, and spoke in a friendly manner. Suspecting no harm, the inmates offered the Indians food, of which they partook. The Indians, seeing some leather thongs in a corner of the room, took the whites by the arms, making signs that they were prisoners, and bound them. Finding it useless to resist against superior force and numbers, they submitted to their fate.

While this was going on up at the Choate cabin, the other party had reached the block-house unobserved. The dogs even failed to give alarm by barking as usual. They were within by the fire instead of being on the watch for their masters' safety. The first notice that the inmates had was that the door was thrown open by a large, resolute Indian, who stepped in by its side to keep it open, while his comrades without rushed in and, with gun and tomahawk, despatched the white men around the fire. Zebulon Throop, who had just returned from the Wolf Creek mill with a bag of meal, was frying meat, and was shot, falling dead into the fire. Several others fell dead at the first discharge and those who survived were disposed of by the tomahawk. No effectual resistance was made, so sudden and unexpected was the attack; but a stout, resolute, backwoods Virginia woman, the wife of Isaac Meeks, who was employed as their hunter, seized an axe and made a blow at the head of the Indian who opened and held the door. A slight turn of the head saved his skull, and the axe passed down through his cheek into his shoulder, leaving a huge gash that severed nearly half his face. Before she could repeat the blow she was killed by the tomahawk of one of the other Indians. This was the only injury received by the savages, as the men were all killed before they had time to get at their arms, which were standing in the corners of the room and out of reach.

While the slaughter was going on, John Stacy, a young man in the prime of life, sprang up the ladder into the upper story and from thence to the roof, hoping in that way to escape, while his brother, Philip, a boy of 16, hid himself under some bedding in the corner of the room. The Indians on the outside, discovering John on the roof, shot him while he was begging them to spare his life, as he was the only one left. The noise made by John upon the roof was heard by the two Bullards, who occupied the lower cabin, and who, hearing the firing at the blockhouse, ran out to learn the cause.

Discovering the Indians around the house, they sprang back into the hut and seized their guns and put to the woods. They had barely left when their door was burst open by the savages. The Indians failed to pursue them, although they knew they had just left.

After the slaughter was over, and scalps secured, one of the important acts in the warfare of the American Indians, they proceeded to collect the plunder. In removing the bedding, the boy, Philip Stacy, was found. Their tomahawks were instantly raised for his destruction, when he throw himself at the feet of the leading warrior and begged for his protection. The savage interposed his authority and saved young Stacy's life. After removing everything they thought valuable, they tore up the floor, piled it over the dead bodies, and set it on fire, thinking to consume the block-house with the carcasses of their enemies. The structure, being made of green beech logs, would not readily burn, and the fire only destroyed the floors and roof, leaving the walls still standing.

In this attack there were 12 persons killed, viz.: John Stacy, Ezra Putnam, John Camp, Zebulon Throop, Jonathan Farwell, James Crouch, William James. John Clark, Isaac Meeks, his wife and two children. The two Choates, Francis and Isaac; Thomas Shaw, young Philip Stacy and James Patton were carried off as prisoners to the British post at Maumee Rapids in the northwest part of this state. Young Stacy died at the Rapids; Patton was adopted into an Indian family and retained until the peace of 1795. The two Choates were ransomed and finally reached their former homes in Massachusetts.

These men in the block-house were all well armed, and no doubt could have defended themselves against the Indians had they only taken proper precautions. But they lacked a proper experienced leader to plan and direct their operations. If they had picketed their house and kept regular guard, the Indians probably would not have ventured an attack; but, seeing the naked block-house, they were encouraged to attempt its capture, and the settlers, apprehending no danger, particularly at that season of the year, did not profit by any advice given them.

The two Bullards, after effecting their escape, traveled rapidly down the river about four miles to Samuel Mitchell's hunting cabin, somewhere about the mouth of Meigs Creek. Captain Rogers, a Revolutionary soldier and a fine hunter, and Dick Layton, a Mohican Indian, were living with Mitchell.

Mitchell was absent at the Mills and Rogers and Dick were lying, wrapped up in their blankets, sleeping by the fire, when they were aroused and made acquainted with the probable fate of the block-house people. Seizing their weapons without delay, they crossed the river on the ice and shaped their course thru the woods for Wolf Creek, distant about six miles, and reached there by 10 o'clock in the night.

The people at the Mills, about 30 in number, were notified of the doings of the savages at Big Bottom, and Samuel Mitchell was dispatched early in the night to give the alarm to the people at Waterford, and two runners were sent to Marietta. The escape of the two Bullards saved the settlers at Wolf Creek Mills and Waterford. If these men had been killed or captured, the Indians would that night have fallen on the unsuspecting inhabitants in their sleep and perhaps have killed all of them. This would have been their fate as the Indians fitted out the war party with the express object of destroying these settlements, and had said that before the leaves again covered the trees they would not leave a smoke of the white man on this side of the Ohio river.

The next day, or January 4th, Captain Rogers led a party of men over to Big Bottom. As the earth was frozen on the outside, a hole was dug within the walls of the house, and the bodies buried in one common grave.

The Indians engaged in this massacre were Delawares and Wyandots, and from the best information subsequently gathered from the prisoners, were about 25 in number. The big Indian wounded by Mrs. Meeks in the door of the block-house, by careful attention finally recovered. If he had died, it was determined upon by his comrades that Francis Choate, one of the prisoners, should be sacrificed as an offering to his spirit, and fulfill their law of revenge.

No further attempt at a settlement was made at Big Bottom until after the peace of 1795. Big Bottom forms as quiet, peaceful and productive an agricultural district as can now be found anywhere on the borders of the Muskingum. After peace came to the county and security was vouchsafed to all settlers, Big Bottom and neighborhood became thronged with immigrants from the east. Among the most prominent and numerous families on the Bottom, and in the township, are remembered as the Cheadles, Davises, Notts, Evelands, Emersons, Ellises, Blackmers, Vancleifs, Newtons, Coburns, Henerys, Whites, Websters and Smiths. Scarcely any of these first settlers are to be found within the township, and but few of their progeny now occupy the soil of Big Bottom or Windsor township.

All of the old pioneers are dead and troops of them years ago sold out and emigrated to the west, making way for a more enterprising and progressive race of agriculturalists and business men.

Celebration of the 4th of July, 1820

The Fourth of July, like Christmas, comes but once a year; and as Christmas is the natal day of the Savior of mankind, so is the 4th of July the birthday of American freedom; while the one deserves and receives the appropriate observance of all Christian people, so the other should be respected and duly celebrated by all American patriots. The 4th of July, 1873, has come and gone, and we apprehend but few of our people hereabouts found with it unusual enjoyments, pleasures or excitements. Our people at this date may be set down as opposed to what is known as the old fashioned way of celebrating that anniversary. In the olden times (it is now near one hundred years since the Declaration of Independence was first proclaimed to the world) it was the fashion to observe the day by appropriate oration, reading the Declaration of Independence, with procession of all the people, old and young, male and female, firing of salutes at the break of day and at the going down of the sun, illuminations and bonfires in the evening, a general suspension of business and an immense amount of noise and general confusion by Young America. We have but few holidays and, in fact, we have too few of them. In the old countries holidays are numerous, and many of them arbitrarily imposed by church, state and societies.

The Fourth of July is our only strictly national anniversary, and should be demonstrated and celebrated in a becoming manner. Coming as it does but once a year, our people can well afford the time and expense in its enjoyment. Times are now not as they once were. It may be said by some that in this Fourth of July business we, as a people, have progressed, not retrograded. This may be a correct position, but it looks as though we have become so selfish that we cannot appreciate that which is known as the love of country; which is the most generous and honorable impulse of a true American heart. The fastidious stand up and ridicule and laugh over what is called the "Spread Eagleism" and extravagances of the day. In their canting way they may have appeared to have forgotten that we are Americans, and we have a history more splendid and honorable than that of any nation upon the face of the earth.

The Fourth of July is our national Sabbath, and the pioneer settlers of McConnelsville and vicinity so considered it and observed the day in its annual return by appropriate demonstrations, so far as the times and the means at hand would permit.

We were then among the woods, brush, stumps and logs, and could not have everything as we desired. We demonstrated in our own way and to our own satisfaction. The day was duly celebrated in the usual old fashioned manner as before that day had been observed by our patriotic forefathers.

The Fourth of July, 1820, was ushered in by the firing of thirteen salutes from an anvil at Price's blacksmith shop, on the west side of Main street, south of Young's tavern. A sumptuous dinner was provided by Mr. James Young and eaten under a bowery which was erected on the lot where the town hall now stands, and directly opposite and east of his hotel. About 200 guests enjoyed the repast, with the presence of several ladies and numerous youngsters, male and female, all of them trimmed off in their best bibs and togas.

At this demonstration there was a feature unseen and unknown at the present day celebrations. It was the presence, in conspicuous position, both in procession and at the table, of some ten or twelve Revolutionary soldiers, invited and honored guests.

About 12 o'clock a procession under the direction of the marshal of the day, and his aides, was formed on the public square, and William Spurgeon with his fiddle and Jonas Fox with his fife, marched (where marching could be done) first up Main street until intercepted by the forest at the corner of the present school house grounds; then countermarched to the square; then down Center street, avoiding stumps, brush-heaps and fallen timber to the river in view of the unpretending and peaceful little village of Malta; then counter-marched to the square; from thence down Main street to the bowery, where those participating in the festivities of the day arranged themselves on each side of the tables, patiently awaiting the order to "pitch in."

The music on this occasion, as may be judged, proved both melancholy and lively; slow and fast; soft and harsh. Two favorite national airs, "Hail, Columbia," and "Yankee Doodle," were alternately played, first upon the fiddle and then upon the fife.

At that day the celebrators were at a loss for much artillery, out of which to make a noise, which was considered an important and essential accompaniment on such occasions. To obviate this difficulty, the marshal of the day was directed to invent something out of which to make the necessary noise. With the materials at hand, he caused to be dug out among the dog-fennel and butter-weeds, which then abounded in the streets, a ditch about ten feet long and two feet in depth, and with a platoon of eight or ten men, equally arranged on each side of the ditch, armed with old late war flint lock muskets, heavily loaded with powder and tow-wads, were discharged into the bottom of this ditch, directed in their exercises by a signal from the president of the day. When the usual toasts on such occasions were to be read and drank, and the proper signal given to the gunners a volley was let loose into the ditch, making a noise equal to a sixpounder; at least, explosions of the guns and boisterous huzzas of the multitude gave satisfaction to those present. In those days, they had their dead-heads. The musicians and those who made the gun-powder noise thru the day and night were furnished with complimentaries to the feast.

Then it was that the Fourth of July was looked upon as a great day—a day of jubilee—when all were free and permitted to express their opinion by speech and sentiment, and no one was allowed to take offense or call in question the exercise of that right. It was the proud day of all the freemen, and they assembled to enjoy themselves, and they did it in their own way and according to their liking.

The repast was gotten up in the then style of the day; the tables groaned with the best the country could afford, and the liquor used was included in the bill of fare and used by all, but not to excess. After the feast, the cloth was removed and the boards were plentifully spread with decanters of liquor and buckets of cool spring water, with the green drinking glasses.

Neither the name of the orator of the day, nor the reader of the Declaration of Independence is now remembered. It is believed, however, that no such persons put in appearance that day, except that the schoolmaster, finding a copy of the Declaration of Independence, was called upon during the day to read the same to the audience, previous to the delivery of the toasts. After the performance of the schoolmaster, the reading and responding to the 13 regular toasts were first in order; after that, came the volunteers thick and fast, containing sentiments of unalloyed patriotism, sallies of keen wit, and biting sarcasm. The proceedings of the day were presided over by a president, who was seated at the head of the table, assisted by a vice president, seated at the foot. It was the duty of the president to call the attention of the guests to the reading of the toasts.

In a loud voice he proclaimed, "Gentlemen, you will now fill your glasses for the first regular toast." The same order was repeated by the vice president, and so continued until the whole 13 were read and applauded.

It was then the decanters and green glasses were heard to jingle, followed with the explosion of the guns in the ditch and the huzzas of the men and Young America. Boys in those days learned from the oration of the Orator, the reading of the Declaration of Independence, and the sentiments offered by the celebrators, the causes that impelled the struggle for liberty; the trials, sufferings and sacrifices of our forefathers, and the triumphant termination and good fruits resulting from that great struggle.

Now, our youth are ignorant of the causes and the results of that great political revolution, which prominently recognized freedom of speech and action to every American citizen, and demonstrates that other great political truth that men everywhere are capable of self-government and should, therefore, make and enforce law.

The regular toasts were thirteen in number, prepared in advance by a committee and read at the table by the president and vice president, and properly noted and observed by the celebrators. As near as can now be remembered, after the lapse of more than half a century, the following regular toasts were given, perhaps not in their regular order and form as then read, but as near as can be.

The Toasts

1st: The day we celebrate; may it never be forgotten.

2nd: The United States; their destiny is in the future, their empire unlimited.

3rd: General George Washington. (Drunk standing and in silence).

4th: The friendly powers throughout the world; may they emulate our example.

5th: The constitution of the United States; the palladium of our liberties.

6th: The President and his Cabinet and the prevailing era of good feeling.

7th: The memory of those who have fallen in defense of American freedom.

8th: Patriots and heroes of the late war.

9th: Agriculture and Commerce, Arts and Sciences. By the former we thrive; by the latter we arise.

10th: Our glorious little Army and Navy; they have done nobly and have taught Old England and her savage allies that a brave and free people cannot be subjugated.

11th: Jackson, Ripley, Scott and Brown, Decatur, Bainbridge, Hull and Jones; heroes by land and sea in the late struggle with proud old England; they deserved the everlasting anthems of a free people.

12th: Woman; man's companion and comforter; they are duly appreciated.

13th: The boys of McConnelsville; wild colts make the best horses when well broken.

The festivities and exercises of the day were closed by a brilliant ball in the evening at Larrison's tavern, sign of "The Buck," located upon the lot now occupied by Cochran & Co.'s work shops, on the corner of Main and Water streets. Balls in those days were attended by the young folks and some of the old, of the village and vicinity. The dancing exercises commenced at four o'clock in the afternoon and continued until "broad daylight in the morning," and with Amasa Piper and his fiddle, his politeness and patience, the dancers hugely enjoyed themselves. In those days of country dances, such as Hornpipes, French and Square Fives, Virginia Reel, etc (cotillions and the various polkas and waltzes of the present day were then unknown to our lads and lassies), the dancers danced to lively tunes with vigorous exercise for at least twelve hours; then the boys and girls went home, not to rest, but to work hard; the boys in the fields and workshops and the girls over the wash-tubs, with the loom, the spinning wheel, breaking flax, and all kinds of housework. As the German exclaimed when speaking of the Americans, "Mein Gott, what a peoples."

The Hunter, The Trapper, The Spy

There were some things connected with the settlements of the western wilds worthy of note at this date. Its history is not altogether a blank in the stirring events of the then turbulent condition of the world, but is highly interesting, and if fully understood and clearly appreciated, will prove instructive to those now far distant in times from those scenes and events.

The first settlers in the country west of the mountains were generally hunters and trappers, with the employed spy as their companion. This class of adventurers made their locations at favorable points here in the vast wilderness, and erected their rude huts and stations. With his rifle and traps and, perhaps, a faithful dog, he found himself alone in the woods, depending upon his own energy and skill for a livelihood. The hunter, in his seclusion from civilization, supported himself by hunting, trapping and fishing. The proceeds of the gun and trap he disposed of to traders and merchants for such articles that were absolutely necessary, such as powder, lead, knives, flints, and a little money; sometimes he procured tobacco and liquor. The merchants, for safety, located themselves and deposited their goods at some friendly post, accessible to the hunter, and from which traders were sent out to look up customers. These frontiersmen or backwoodsmen, as they were called, were an independent class of men, and at a very remote day commenced their operations along the western slopes of the Alleghenies, gradually advancing west and southwest into the wilderness as emigration and civilization crowded upon them. They were a sort of advance guard, and in every particular a remarkable class of men. In their far-off haunts they were without law and under no restraints, but for self-security and protection they agreed to observe towards one another certain unwritten rules and regulations, the strict compliance with which prevented unpleasant collisions, broils and deadly strife. Each hunter, by his own choice, had his field of range upon which to operate, and these bounds he claimed as his own for the purposes for which he appropriated them. In that particular locality he was monarch of the domain; no one to molest him or make him afraid, except the wily, lurking Indian who disregarded his claim and on frequent occasions would fall upon the unprotected hunter and rob him of his furs and accumulated spoils.

Many, very many, were the unrecorded deadly strifes and contests between the original proprietor and the squatter.

After permanent peace had come to the country and the Indian title to the lands had been settled by treaty; then followed the surveying and sale of the public lands, causing large immigration and settlements pretty generally along the watercourses and in the most fertile and choice locations. This great flow of emigrants, men of limited means who, with their families, had left the eastern states, came along gradually and perceptibly disturbed the occupations and business of the old frontiersmen. So great was this intrusion of these settlers upon the hunting grounds of the old hunters, driving before them and destroying, without the observance of any rules of economy, the deer, elk, buffalo, beaver, otter, and other valuable peltries, that in 1819 but few of them had an abiding place in the country hereabouts.

Now and then there might be met with one of these original characters who still lingered, reluctant to depart from his old haunts of sport, pleasure and profit, notwithstanding the innovations and advantages made by the more civilized and refined.

These trappers and hunters, and those who, in the early conflicts with the savages, were employed and acted as spies, were a brave and active class of men, of close observation, quick perception and prompt action. They were well informed in all that pertained to the habits, customs and manners of the Indians.

As these frontiersmen would go along on their scouts, tramps and forays through the unbroken wilderness, nothing would escape their observation, and whatever they would see or hear, they could immediately account for.

If anything mysterious should present itself, they would stop and not move until it was solved to their satisfaction. When on a trail they would stop and stand still for hours to account for certain traces or effects in tracks that might present themselves. These men, when trailing, would carry the head somewhat inclined forward, intent on the object before them, with a quick and restless eye always on the lookout and hardly ever crossing the track of man or animal without seeing it and making observations.

The spy, who was an important character, and a great help to the very early settlers of the country, and one whose services were much needed and could not well be dispensed with, could tell by observation and long practice of his art all the peculiarities of the signs in the trail he might fall upon. In his tramps thru the woods he might fall upon the tracks of an Indian horse; he will follow it a few miles and without coming up with it, ascertain it to have been that of a "stray black horse, with a long, bushy tail, nearly starved to death, has a split hoof of the left forefoot, and goes very lame, and passed that point early in the morning." He ascertained all these particulars by close observation of the tracks of the horse, and other signs, as he followed along the trail. He knows it to be a stray horse because it did not go in a straight or direct course; it's tail was long and bushy because he dragged it over the snow, and in brushing his tail against the bushes he left some hairs which showed the horse to be black; the horse he knew to be hungry for, in going along, it nipped at high, dry weeds which horses seldom eat; the break in the left fore-foot left, also, its track, and the depth of the indentation shows the degree of its lameness, and the tracks show that he went along in the morning when the snow was hard with frost. Again, he comes across the track of an Indian; he takes his observations and minutely examines same with his practiced eye. He decides him to be an old Delaware Indian who is out to look after his traps in the vicinity. He decides that the Indian carried in his right hand a trap and in his left hand a lasso to catch a horse he had lost. He ascertains, by certain evidences in the tracks, that the Indian returned without the horse, but that he had caught in his trap a wolf, which he carried home on his back, and a bundle of kinikinick wood in his right hand.

The trailer will tell you that he knows that the Indian is old by the impressions and slips his gait has made, and that he is a Delaware by his moccasins. The trap he carried struck the snow now and then, and still carrying the trap in the same manner shows that he did not find the horse. Drops of blood in his tracks showed that he carried the wolf on his back, and the bundle of kinikinick wood he used as a staff for support; and catching a wolf showed that he had traps. He knew that it was not a fox or any small game that he carried, for if it were he would have slipped the head of the animal in his waist belt, and so carried it by his side and not on his shoulder; it was not a deer, for they are not caught by traps. He meets with other Indian tracks; he puts his woodsman's wits to work to ferret out the designs of the fellow, and what he is after. He decides that "he is an Indian prowling about to steal horses, carried a rifle gun, and had killed some white man lately and had passed along there one week ago." He knew these things from the signs before him, for a lone Indian in this part of the country, he decides, is on mischief, and looking for a chance to stel a horse. He had on the shoes of a white man, whom he had in all probability killed, but his tracks, he knows, are those of an Indian, for the toes turn in, while a white man's turn out. Passing across a hollow, the end of his gun hit the deep snow, showing a single barrel—therefore, a rifle gun.

A week before that it had been a very warm day and the snow being then soft made the tracks deep down, and since then the weather had been intensely cold, the tracks were made shallow.

The Indian never buys shoes, and those worn must have been taken from the feet of a white man, and if the Indian did buy them he would not have bought them as large as these were for the Indians have very small feet.

From these men, much valuable information might be obtained, as to the character of the soil, the geography and topography of the country and the most desirable points of location in the territory. These men were somewhat reticent, but at times seeing an interest taken by the interviewer in their history and varied careers, would become communicative, and the chances, perils and profits of hunting, trailing and trapping were themes upon which they delighted to dwell.

In the last chapter an attempt is made to give the character of the hunter, trapper and trailer, who found an early home and occupation here in the western wilderness.

At a later day, say some 60 or more years ago, out of some half dozen or more old hunters who delighted to follow in the chase, and whose lives were principally devoted to the business of hunting and trapping, we find quite prominent, Abe Hughes, who, with his brother, Bill, had located themselves among the hills of upper Wolf Creek.

Abe and Bill could not be brought to adopt all the customs and habits of their more civilized neighbors, who gradually extended and settled about them. These intrusive neighbors came into the country for an entirely different purpose than that followed by the Hugheses and their contemporaries.

The Indian having disappeared from the country and under treaty surrendered his title to the soil to the government; surveys of the land into small tracts being completed; sales of land constantly going on at the government land office, emigration followed. These emigrants came to open up the country, to develop its resources, and find for themselves and their children, homes and contentment. Abe and Bill became restless by being thus circumscribed in the limits of their hunting grounds, and in disturbing the solitude and stillness of the forest by that great leveler, the axe, which in the hands of the sturdy pioneer woodsman was the instrument to conquer the forest, open up farms, build towns and cities. It was the introduction of the axe in place of the rifle and traps, yet the rifle was still the companion of the settler, either suspended in his cabin or in his hand when on the chase.

The old hunters lingered among us as long as they could well bear with the intruders. Finally, they took up their rifles and traps, being about the amount of their worldly goods, and departed on the trail of his red man, towards the setting sun, to find a more plentiful and unmolested range for the pursuit of their favorite operations.

A description of the dress of one of the old hunters, as presented to the view of the early settler, may suffice for all such as were found here upon the Muskingum river 60 or more years ago. Take Abe Hughes as a fair sample of the illustrious race of hunters, and one who was last to leave his old haunts, and the reader will understand something about them, their appearance and their dress. In addition to the Hugheses may be remembered as old hunters and early frontiersmen, and spies and trailsmen, Dan Bean, Dave Fouts, Old Man Choate, and others, who lingered behind to watch with no great degree of approval the rapid advances of civilzation and improvement made by the intruders who had squatted down here and there among them.

Abe Hughes, our hero in this sketch, in his person would be noticed and marked by the most careless observer. He stood full six feet, with long legs, long arms and long neck; with an Adam's apple in his throat in size equal to the crook of the first point of the forefinger of the largest hand, head thrown back, making the apple of his throat more prominent and as conspicuous as the nose on his face, which was immense, Roman shaped, knocked a little to one side by some unlucky blow received in some of his fisticuff tournaments at which exercises every hunter and backwoodsman was expected to be proficient, whether he had occasion to thus indulge himself or not. He was coarse and rough in his ways, yet he possessed, like most of his race, a good heart within, and with a coonskin cap as a winter covering to his head, he personified well the early backwoodsman of the Muskingum.

Abe's other dress was the common costume of the backwoodsman and consisted principally of a tow linen shirt and pantaloons, manufactured at home, with buckskin moccasins, leggings or gaiters, and hunting shirt, killed with his own gun and dressed with his own hands. The moccasins were made to neatly fit his foot, and for the want of woolen socks (sheep were not plentiful here in the woods in those days) dry oak leaves mostly supplied the place of socks and stockings. Above these were placed the leggings or gaiters, made to fit the leg and tie in at the ankle with the moccasins, extending some distance above the knees, and a strap from the upper part extending up and buttoning to the hip of the pantaloons. Leggings were defense against snakes, briars, nettles, etc., for then the rattlesnake, copperhead and other poisonous reptiles abounded in the path of the backwoodsman. In cutting these leggings or gaiters a surplus was left on the outside and at the outer seam. This surplus was from one to two inches in width which, after the seam was sewed, was cut into an ornamental fringe. The buckskin hunting shirt comes next to cover this under-dress; for wool in those days was too scarce to indulge much in the Virginia hunting shirt, which in after days became a very comfortable and common male dress, and ornamented in the same way, with the fringe down the outside of the arms, around the collar, cape, belt and tail, and sometimes down the seams on the arms, and other parts.

It may be thought strange, but nevertheless it is a fact, the hunter in the woods will adhere to fashion, as much as does the dandy in the city. Fashions will reign and rule the human mind more than we're sometimes willing to confess, and as we see in the stately palaces of the city, so in the hut in the woods, these ornaments on the buckskin hunting shirts were carried to excess among the hunters of olden times, whose taste in all other things may be counted on as less refined.

Thus habited, the frontiersman, if he should be ambitious in that direction, thought himself quite sufficiently equipped to attend any kind of a gathering common to the country. Now and then they might be met in the church, the wedding, the dance, and all kinds of social bees observed by the early settlers. At that day a new hunting shirt, leggings and moccasins had upon the fair sex about the same claims to draw forth the approving looks and smiles as in these days when the effeminate beau struts his long tailed black or blue, the dandy dress, or the glittering uniform; and all this approval was not a whit less appreciated by the young buckskin, coming from rosy lasses, who were dressed in linsey-woolsey, cross-barred or Scotch plaid, or, perhaps, partly in buckskin, highly fringed and tastefully ornamented, than they are now, with their silks, laces and artificials. This race of people is gone, and their like may now be found, with the same costumes, habits, and following the same pursuits far off in the west, on the confines of civilization, a sort of link between the white man and Indian.

Some of the men and women who have been raised in this manner upon the frontiers, and their children, who shared with them the dangers, toils and vicissitudes of border life, have, in after days, occupied high public stations, not in their exaltation forgetting former situation in life, but with satisfaction and pleasure referring to and relating the events of the past. These old hunters and trappers and frontiersmen and women, these spies and trailers upon the movements of the wily savages in the days of the gleaming knife, should not now be forgotten, but remembered, and their services to the country fully appreciated.

After the establishment of Morgan county by an act of the general assembly of Ohio in 1818, it became necessary that the county should be organized with a court, and by the appointment of certain county officers, creation of new townships, and the holding of elections. A part of the organization consisted then in the erection of new townships by the county commissioners and the ordering by the court of the election of justices of the peace therein, on a certain day, and, in some instances, designating the place.

The records and files still existing in the clerk's office, furnish evidence of the organization of the townships of Bloom, Bristol, Center, Deerfield, Manchester, Meigsville, Penn, Union, Windsor and York; all within the present bounds of Morgan county and in the years of 1819 and 1820.

It would perhaps be gratifying to the children of the old settlers, and interesting to those who may now sojourn in their places, besides quite desirable for future history and information, that as full and complete a list as possible of the pioneer settlers of the county in the above years of 1819 and 1820 should be obtained and presented. At this day but few persons remain among us who can accurately furnish the names of those adult males who resided here and took part in the affairs of the county and townships so long ago as 1819 and 1820. Scarcely a score of those young, active, enterprising men who came here at an early day and, by their industry and management, commenced to make the wilderness bud and blossom as the rose, have an existence or abiding place among us. Therefore, for more accurate and reliable historical facts, resort is had to those records and files, and from which source a very accurate and full list of the names of our early pioneers and their locations may be procured; and, also, as far as can be, mention is made of those who may survive those early days.

In these lists given, the names of some of the early pioneers may be omitted, but not intentionally; for it must be remembered that the period from which we gather these names is confined to 1819 or a few years subsequent thereto. If there are any omissions, it is for the reason that the sources consulted fail to give them.

Bloom Township

Is here introduced, and from the records and files a pretty complete list of the names of the first settlers is made. As has been stated elsewhere, the first court organized in the county was on the 5th day of April, A. D. 1819. William Rannels, Sherebiah Clark and Wm. B. Young were then the associate judges of the court. The presiding judge, Ezra Osborn, Esq., of Portsmouth, Scioto county, did not put in an appearance until the March term, 1820. At the term (July 7th, 1819) the court caused the following entry to be made upon their journal: "Whereas, it appears to the court that the commissioners of Morgan county have set off a new township, by the name of Bloom. Ordered that said township be entitled to two justices of the peace and that the qualified electors of said township be authorized to elect said justices at the house of Jas. Whitaker within said township, on Saturday, the 24th instant." This order being thus made, such of the qualified electors of the new township of Bloom as seemed to be interested in the result, did, on the 24th day of July, 1819, meet at the house of James Whitaker and organized themselves for the purpose of electing two justices of the peace: Jonathan Frisby, John N. Gibson and Zuriel Sherwood were selected as judges; Wm. Silvey, W. Montgomery as clerks of election. James Whitaker, at whose house this first election was held, then lived upon and owned the farm upon which Richard McElhiney now resides, on the east bank of the river, directly below the Rokeby dam. Thirty-six pioneer electors, being about one-sixth the number of voters now found in the township, appeared and voted at this election. It is supposed that every adult male inhabitant of the township was present at this election. This election being a new thing to the pioneer and there being some interest taken in the same, it is presumed that the old pioneers turned out in their full strength, and it is believed that below we have a full list of them, who lived in Bloom township 55 years ago: John Stutes, Enoch Loper, James McElhiney, Calvin Nott, J. N. Gibson, John Dingman, J. Frisby, Samuel Hammett, James Rogers, M. McElhiney, J. Conway, Wm. Briggs, James Frisby, Daniel Eveland, Z. Sherwood, James Eveland, Robert Slone, David Smith, George Jackson, James Briggs, Peter Secord, A. Whitaker, J. S. Gibson, James Whitaker, James Silvey, Joseph Smith, William Eveland, William Silvey, Thomas James, W. Montgomery, Daniel Swartz, G. Mingus, Nathan Smith, Samuel McCune, Robert McCune, B. Whipple.

At this election, Joseph Smith received 35 votes, David Smith, 18, Samuel McCune, 7, and William Montgomery, 12. Joseph and David Smith were each proclaimed elected and were commissioned accordingly.

In carefully looking over this list of pioneers, not one of them is recognized as living today. Several of them continued to reside in the township until the day of their death; others of them emigrated into the west and have long since been gathered to their fathers. Zuriel Sherwood and William Silvey are, perhaps, the last survivors of the list, both of them deceased within the last year or so. Many of the children of these old first settlers still live in the township and county.

The record and files being further consulted, show that in April, 1820, the following named persons had an abiding place in the township of

Bloom, to-wit: Daniel Bean, Robert Longworth, Andrew Clark, Peter Landerman, J. Spurgeon and Thomas Wells; and in October following, the following old settlers had their names enrolled at a justice's election, viz.: James Stone, Zachariah Cuddington, J. James, James Camp, John Bowers, Robert McCune, Jonathan McMullen, J. Frisby, Jacob Fouts, John Clemens, M. Wilson, William Bennett and Zachariah Lawrence; and again in April, 1823, we find the following named, though some of them had been residents of the township a year or two before, yet this is their first apearance, viz.: Abel Larrison, George Osborn, Samuel Shaw, Joseph Mummey, Robert Ingram, Mounts Nichols, John and William Hammond, Reuben Shilling, Thomas Taylor, William Shivel, David Taylor, G. Crow, Amos Nichols, John Dutro, John Sevall, Moses Largent, Isaac Hanes, J. F. Talley, William White, Samuel Farra, Daniel Lawrence, John H. Livezey, E. Nichols, Daniel Weeks, Caleb Osborn and Andrew McConeha. In October of the same year, the names of the following were recorded, viz.: David Edwards, L. Stedman, William Sherwood, Michel Burns, Thomas White, Greenbury Caton, William Hutcheson and Daniel Weeks.

The above names comprise about a full list of the settlers in Bloom township 50 years ago. Zachariah Cuddington, George Osborn, William Hammond, John F. Talley and William Sherwood are recognized as the only survivors upon these lists.

It will be remembered by those who had knowledge of the early settlers of Bloom in 1819 and 1820 that the largest number of them were confined to and made their settlements along the river; but few of them were found at that period in the hills back from the river. In 1821 and down to the period that settlements were made off the river.

In these recollections one thing must be observed, that, dependent as we now are upon the early election returns for the names of the early settlers, it is presumed some of them did not attend at these elections; therefore, to procure as accurate lists as possible, several poll books, following the first election, must be consulted. Some of the earliest pioneers were of foreign birth and did not attend elections until after their naturalization, and if they settled in the county in 1819, they could not, perhaps, immediately engage in the political organization of the township.

In Bloom township, mention may be made of the Martins, Alfred, Samuel and George; the Morrises, George P. and Edward; Clement Pine, and others not now remembered, who settled in that township as early as 1819 and whose names do not appear in the regular lists for some five or six years thereafter.

Bristol Township

On the 7th day of July, 1819, the court made the following order in regard to the organization of Bristol township.

"Whereas, as it appears that our Commissioners of Morgan county have set off a new township, by the name of Bristol: Ordered that said township be entitled to two justices of the peace; and, whereas, it appears that there is now one acting justice of the peace within said township: Ordered that the qualified electors of said township be authorized to assemble at the house of Mr. Merwin, in said township, on Saturday, the 24th instant, for the purpose of electing one other justice of the peace."

In accordance with this order, the pioneer electors, who took an interest in this election, met and duly organized for the purpose designated, by appointing Jos. Devereaux, Geo. Herring and Lemon Fouts, judges; Ashur Allen and Archibald McCullum, clerks. At this election, there were 24 votes cast, and the judges and clerks, in their certificate of results, declare: "We do hereby certify that Simon ———— is duly elected justice of the peace by a clear vote of the electors." This election was held at the house of Simon Merwin and upon the farm now owned and occupied by George Glenn, Esq.

Bristol township can now give near 12 times as many votes as were at this time cast. It is presumed that this vote for a justice does not present a full list of the pioneers in that township, for there being no opposition to the successful candidate, the vote, therefore, was necessarily light. It appears, however, that at an election held two years afterwards, June 30, 1821, for a justice, there were only 36 votes cast, showing either very little interest, or but a small increase in the settlements.

At the first election the following 24 pioneer voters appeared and, it is believed, none of them survive except Robert Rowland and Richard Jenkins, viz: John Bickford, Andrew Fouts, Samuel Shattuck, Daniel Linsey, Lovitt Bishop, Anderson Underhill, Jared Andrews, Hugh Osborn, Ansel Taylor, Thomas Jenkins, John McCollum, William Rowland, Robert Rowland, Richard Jenkins, David Sproul, Benj. W. Talbott, William Fordice, Archibald McCollum, Joseph Devereaux, Lemon Fouts, George Herring, Asher Allen, Thomas Stevens and John Carlin.

At an election for justice of the peace held June 30, 1821, about two years after the first election, Alexander Martin, David McAllister, Andrew McAllister, Stanton Fordice, James Taylor, Philip Moore, James Davidson, Abraham Davis, Alex. Vaughn, Jesse Gibbs, David Stevens, James Finley, Levi Whaley, John Knox, Dan Martin, John Parmiter, Saml. Fouts, Edmund Murdock, Thomas Nott and John German appeared and for the first time voted.

Afterwards, at an election held in the township in August, 1822, appeared the following additional persons: Chauncey D. Gry, Danl. Prouty, Job Kennison, Lovitt Cady, William Hempfield, Seth Andrews, Wilkes Bozman, Ezra Kennison, Ezra Osborn, Isaac Whitehouse, Peter L. Lupardis, Thomas McGrath, Ebenezer Ellis and Zadock Dickerson.

In 1824, the following additional persons are found upon the record, participating in the affairs of the township, viz: Adrial Huzzey, David Howard, Lot Workman, William Murray, Jonathan P. Lawrence, William Hoyt, Andrew Hosom, Thos. Knox, Charles Davis, James Howard, Mordecai Bishop, Alvin Fuller, Thomas Rowland, Albert G. Grubb, Philip Bonham, William Barr, Thomas Carlin, Daniel Lawrence, Jr., Benjamin Taylor, Uriah Martin, Absolom Fouts, Job Armstrong, and William Bemis.

The above may be taken as containing about a full list of the early settlers of Bristol up to about 1825. The latter portion of these settlers were emigrants from the state of Maine. The Bickfords, Shattucks, Linseys, Andrewses, Osborns, McCollums, Fordices, Allens, Stevens (Thomas), and some others were about the first who came—followed in 1820-21-22 by the Parmiters, Kennisons, McCallisters, Murdocks, Lawrences. Hosoms, Fullers, Holbrooks, Ellises, Whitehouses, McGraths and others not now remembered. Some few Pennsylvanians, Virginians, etc., the Herrings, Rowlands, Howards, Carlins, Taylors, Stevens (David), Moores, Talbotts, Foutses, and others were early emigrants, generally settling along the creeks.

In this township there are two branches of Meigs Creek, together with Horse Run, a branch of Dye's Fork of Meigs Creek, watering all parts of the township; the bottoms of which are exceedingly rich and productive in all the cereals and grasses. The west branch is called Man's Fork and the East branch, which is the middle branch of the creek, is called Boal's Fork, and named after two of the first and most prominent settlers upon their waters.

Bristol township is not only celebrated for its rich and productive soil, but during the last half century it has been quite productive in the way of population. The circumscribed limits of a township, only containing 36 square miles, fails to hold and retain the great increase. For years past the Bristol township population, like all other parts of the county, have been swarming yearly and all the time, and going forth; and everywhere in the west may be found the Bristol boys and girls, contending successfully, in most instances, in the great battles of life. In the list of pioneer settlers of Bristol township we recognize only Robert Rowland, Richard Jenkins, James Taylor, William Hempfield, Isaac Whitehouse, Thomas Knox and James Howard, surviving, and standing monuments of early pioneer life.

There were, perhaps, no people in the pioneer days of the county who enjoyed themselves more rationally and actively 40 and 45 years ago than did the people of "Old Bristol." The Maine Yankees and the Pennsylvania and Virginia corncrackers coming together and commingling at their social gatherings, back-woods fashion, made to themselves lively times.

Numerous laughable anecdotes and interesting scenes and incidents are related as taking place among the pioneers. Edmund Murdock, Zera Patterson, the Devols, Fordices, Lawrences, Foutses, Wellses and others, all young and active men, were prominent characters at that day, actively engaging in all enterprises, athletic exercises and social gatherings, such as house raisings, log-rollings, corn-shuckings, balls, quiltings, dances, and then, too, they were prominent at church, weddings and funerals. While under the "stated preaching" of Rev. Elder Adrial Huzzey at "Old Bristol Meeting House" (the only place of worship in the Twp. for years) the people were mildly reproved for their transgressions and timely advised as to how they should conduct themselves one to another, making themselves acceptable in the sight of that "Divinity Who shapes our ends, rough-hew them as we will."

Bristol township, with all its enterprise, energy and wealth, so prominently manifested in its whole history, has failed to build up any considerable village within its borders. The only place of note to be found in the township is the village of Bristol, laid out by Thomas Stevens 1831, containing in its survey about 14 lots, with the necessary roads and lanes running through it for the convenience of its inhabitants and stock.

This village is located on the state road leading from McConnelsville to Barnesville, and about seven miles from the former place, and is the great central business point of the township. It is in the suburbs of this village, where stood for more than half of a century the old Bristol meeting house, about the first house built in the county for public worship. This old church was a free church, open to the use and occupancy of all denominations of Christians, to all political parties, and all kinds of legitimate and proper gatherings; but like many other things of old and pure origin, it has been made to give way to the age of improvement and progress, and the place where the old Bristol meeting house so long stood as a conspicuous landmark now yields to the invasion of the ruthless plow and the tramp of the unheeding husbandman.

This village of Bristol failed to flourish and spread itself to that extent as contemplated by its venerable and public spirited proprietor. Some envious and evil disposed person, full of expedients to blast the good name, fame and prospects anticipated by the embryo village, and being moved in his hatred and ill will by that evil spirit that at times seems to have control of the human heart, put into circulation a report that some of its inhabitants had a fondness for the taste of mutton, and mutton they would have, whether in a legitimate way or not. These outside barbarians who had lost their mutton, instead of leaving their ninety and nine unlost sheep and going forth in a friendly way in search of the lost one, in their hatred and contempt of the villagers, gave the town, just blooming into importance and notice, the contemptible and mean name of "Muttonburg" and by which name it is now known far and near, and will so continue to be known and called, it is feared, until the Angel Gabriel sounds his last trump. So much for a name and its origin.

Center Township

In continuation of the list of pioneers in Morgan county of 54 years ago, the township of Center comes next in order.

The county commissioners struck off the new township of Center, and the court, at their session July 6th, 1819, ordered that the qualified voters of the township be authorized to elect two justices of the peace for said township, on Saturday, July 17, 1819. The election was not held the day ordered, but on the 24th day of July, 1819, and with Philander Andrews, Adkin Waterman and John Laughery, Judges; Phineas Coburn and Enoch S. McIntosh, clerks, the people assembled and proceeded to hold the election. There were 26 votes given at this election, and Lot Guard, having received 25 of them, was declared elected. It appears there was only one justice of the peace elected instead of two ordered, and from the future contests in the township it would seem that this election was held null and void and of no effect.

The pioneer electors at this, the first election in the township, were: George Nott, Forest Belknap, James McManes, Cyrus Andrews, Job West, John Tope, David Stevens, Peter L. Lupardies, Enoch S. McIntosh, Jason Andrews, John Coay, Lot Guard, Nicholas Hoyt, Patrick Sherlock, George Bentley, Daniel Scott, Wm. L. Ireland, John Laughery, Philander Andrews. John Perry, Phineas Coburn, Adkin Waterman, Saml. McMara, David Fulton, Samuel Sailor and Elisha Griswold.

About these times the old pioneers had lively and exciting times in Center township over their elections for justice of the peace. In April, 1821, Enoch S. McIntosh was elected one of the justices. This election appears to have been legally held, and remained undisturbed; but in October, 1822, an election was held for two justices, James Anderson, Nathan Newton and Joseph C. Linn, judges; Phineas Coburn and Samuel Waterman, clerks.

Forty votes were cast. James Anderson received 29 votes, Lot Guard 25, Joseph C. Linn 15, Phineas Coburn 3, John P. Anderson 1, and David Scott 1. The legality of this election was questioned and contested. S. A. Barker, clerk of the court, made the following endorsement upon the poll book: "Contested and set aside in consequence of a candidate, to-wit, James Anderson, being a judge of election and a foreigner."

Another election was ordered and held on the 3rd day of November, 1822. John Brown, David Scott and Adin Waterman, judges, and Phineas Coburn and Hiram J. L. Brown, clerks. At this election there were only 27 votes polled. Two justices were to be elected. Lot Guard received 14 votes, Joseph C. Linn 17, Nathan Newton 4, and Wm. Oliphant 18. It appears by the files that this election was not held according to law, and a contest, on complaint, was had. On the contest, a report was made to the court of the court of common pleas, emanating from both the contestor and the committee of freeholders selected to hear and report upon the case. The report may be of some interest to the present people of Center township. It is therefore given in full, showing the way in which our old pioneer voters sometimes did up their business. No doubt they were honest but awkward, both in their chirography and spelling, and due allowance must, therefore, be made in this case, for the common school system, now so prevalent, had no existence at that day in Ohio. What little education our pioneer boys and girls got at that day was doled out to them through subscription schools few and far between, held only during the winter months. Scarcely a church and not a public school house coul.1 be found in the land. The following is the report:

'We the onder siners beingen cold apond and sworn akorden to law to exemen the contested Lection of Joseph C. Lin and William Olephan of Senter Townshep the Advertisen on legal and the lection being closed be for fore aclok these pints bein proving to our Satersfacon.—Henry Taylor, Contestor. Zephania Tyson, Henry Nichels, Robert Welch, 2nd J. P."

After this failure another election was called, and then came the tug of war among the friends of the several aspirants. The pioneer voters seemed to have rallied from all parts of the township, greatly excited and intensely interested in the result. At this election 50 votes were cast. Adin Waterman, Jonathan Penny and Hiram J. L. Brown acted as judges, and Phineas Coburn and Benj. Guard as clerks. Lot Guard received 23 votes, Nathan Newton 6, William Oliphant 27, Joseph Linn 30, and P. Coburn and John Brown 1 vote each. This poll book was returned to the clerk's office and the clerk summoned two justices of the peace to open the same and make certification of the result. They certified "that Joseph C. Linn was duly elected, and is entitled to a commission accordingly."

The justices also certified that "by the poll book it appears that Wm. Oliphant is the next highest in number but there is nothing in the poll book to show that the election was held for the purpose of electing more than one justice." N. B.—In this case the clerk was in favor of declaring two justices elected.

This election appears to have ended the bitter strifes and contests among the old pioneer settlers of Center township, so far as the same applied to their local courts of justice. Without further examining into this matter, it is supposed both Linn and Oliphant were duly commissioned, as the number of votes counted out to each is evidence sufficient to show that the electors voted for two justices. Joseph C. Linn, one of the successful candidates in this exciting and protracted struggle, afterwards became an associate judge of the county, and now resides with his son, D. B. Linn, Esq., near Zanesville, at an advanced age, and enjoying good health. William Oliphant died at his residence in Center township some years since.

In 1822, when a large vote was given, it is presumed that several of those who then voted were residents of the township in 1819 but did not take sufficient interest in that contest to come out. We recognize as, perhaps, among the earliest settlers, Peter and Joseph Keith, Thomas Taylor, Alva Hoyt, Abraham, Daniel and Jonathan Penney, William Burrows, John Brown, William Bailey, Nathan Newton, William Laughery, Ambrose Elliott, Richard Kay, Edward Petty, Abigah C. Serley, Joseph Serley, Jason Payne, J. C. Linn, Abraham Smith, and John P. Anderson.

Of all the list of early settlers of Center, Joseph C. Linn, of Zanesville, and Enoch S. McIntosh, of Beverly, are the only ones known to be now living. They are both quite aged.

Among the list of early pioneers will be recognized Mr. Abraham Smith. Smith was an old wolf hunter and trapper, and went by the name of "Wolf Smith" to distinguish him among the numerous families of Smiths. After the wolf business had become slack and unprofitable, the old gentleman turned his attention to the distillation of all kinds of essences common to the country. Among his neighbors he took the name of "Essence Smith," and so continued in his good work of distilling perfumery until his death several years ago.

Center township is extensively watered by Big and Little Olive Green Creeks. The bottoms of these creeks and tributaries are well adapted to the production of Indian corn, and perhaps no better corn lands can be found in the county. The hill lands are good for all kinds of fruit. Several large fruit orchards are to be found on the high ground of that township.

Olive Green Creek derived its name from Robert Oliver and Griffen Green, early settlers at Marietta, and who first explored the country through which the creek runs. They were directors of the Ohio Company's Purchase.

In April, 1823, other pioneers make their appearance for the first time in the business transactions of the township, viz: Isaac, Richard and Israel Ross, Samuel Clogston, Isaac Jordan, Daniel Chidester, John and Lewis Carter, Nathaniel Chapman, Joseph McKinley, John Phillis, James and Alexander Conn, and John Kepple. Some of these, perhaps, with others named, had made settlements in the township at an earlier day, but the records consulted fail to show the period of their emigration; they only show the time when they first appear participating in their township transactions.

Manchester Township

There are no files or records found going to show when and how Manchester township was set off as a township of Morgan county, but it appears that the inhabitants of that township lived together from the first organization of the county in 1819 up to August, 1822, without law, legal organization, justice, or anything else indicating a political existence. It is supposed that such a state of affairs among a busy, active and enterprising people as were the first settlers became intolerable, and the inhabitants, who by this time had become quite numerous—for then Manchester contained a territory of 36 square miles—(since then the east half has been lost to Morgan and incorporated into the new county of Noble), petitioned the court of common pleas of Morgan county to place them in a position where the evils complained of and existing among them might be remedied and that they might have a position among the civilized communities of the earth worthy of a free people. The court, therefore, on Monday, July 11, 1822, with a full bench of judges, made the following order:

"Whereas, it appears that no justices of the peace have been allowed for Manchester township; it is therefore ordered that said township be entitled to two justices of the peace; and the qualified electors of said township meet at the usual place of holding elections in said township, at such time as the trustees may direct, and proceed to elect two justices for said township."

Without delay an election was ordered to be held on the 3rd day of August, 1822. Accordingly on that day the pioneer voters of Manchester convened at some point in the township, not now remembered by the oldest inhabitant, and proceeded to organize and hold the election, by selecting Nathan Smith, John Eddy and Benjamin Deen, judges, and David Fulton and Lewis G. Harding, clerks. At that election, there were 45 votes cast, viz: David Devore, Andrew Matheney, Enoch Deen, William Ellison, Thomas Gregg, William Sherman, Nathan Dimmick, Ephraim Echerman, Charles Harward, Peter Moler, Samuel Sprague, James Matheney, John Skivington, Joseph Echerman, David Fulton, Jonathan Rex, Henry Mohler, Jacob Teeters, Lewis G. Harding, Nathan Smith, Samuel Sailors, John Gregg, John Sears, John Eddy, Benjamin Deen, William McNabb, James Geddes, William Sprague, William McNabb, Sr., Michael Kuntz, John Tope, Aaron Sprague, Jonathan Sprague, Philip

Swank, Enos Deen, Robert Caldwell, Alexander Echerman, Archibald Gregg, William Brown, Cyrus Echerman, Nathan Essex, William Swank, John Swank, and James Conn.

On counting out the votes, it appeared that John Sears received 36 votes, John Gregg 44, and Richard Dore 8. Sears and Gregg were declared duly elected and commissioned. Not one of these 45 pioneer voters who then participated in the organization of Manchester township are known to be alive except, perhaps, Robert Caldwell, of Sharon township, Noble county. Several of their children, however, still reside in the bounds of the township and in the county, with many of them emigrating to populate and build up the west.

The Rexes, Greggs, Harwards, Molers, Spragues, Teeterses, Sailors, McNabbs, Matheneys, Clinginsmiths, Swanks, Kuntzes, Echermans, Geddeses, Conns, Clarks, and some others are now remembered as the most prominent and numerous families among the early pioneers of the original township of Manchester.

Jonathan Rex, with his mill, stillhouse and general enterprise, for a long time was acknowledged a leading character of the township, and his death, several years since, was much regretted by his old friends and companions in the early settlements of the country.

That part of old Manchester township still left to us in Morgan is not recognized to be very rich and productive. There are, however, many acres of most excellent land upon Dye's Fork of Meigs Creek and Little Olive Green, the one running through the township on the west and the other skirting along the east border. The uplands are inviting, and with proper care and attention, and suitable seasons, produce well in most of crops suitable to the soil.

In 1825 there are found in the original township of Manchester the following named settlers. These pioneers turned out to an election that was held for two justices of the peace, when Robert Jackson and John Sears were elected. There is no doubt that the most of them had settlement in Manchester township years before this, their first appearance here, but the precise year they came into the township cannot be ascertained from the records consulted, viz: John Needham, Jacob Hawk, John Wimor, Edward Trimbel, John M. Sears, Palsor and Adam Keith, Philip and Jacob Swank, David Clinginsmith, John Conkle, William T. Jordon, James D. Matheney, John and Peter Kuntz, Washington Stewart, Benjamin Harding, William and Samuel McClintock, Edmond and Ebenezer Dimmock, Samuel, George and John Brown, Henry Teeter, John Crooks, Peter and John Pickingpaugh, Jacob Swank, Absolom and Morgan Maxwell, Mahlon and David Wilson, James Gregg, Alfred Sears, Obediah Ellison, John and Abraham Shuster, George Anthony, Peter Shackle, John Whitmore, Jas. Archibald, George Gion, Henry Hartman, Edward O'Harra and Joseph Chalk.

Edward O'Harra, whose name appears among the list of the early pioneers of Manchester township, was a well known character. "Chartered Ned," as he was called, is no doubt still remembered by many of those now living in the township of Manchester in Morgan county, and Sharon, Noble county. Old Ned was prominent at all kinds of gatherings common at that time among the early settlers. One incident used to be related by Gen. Alexander McConnell, somewhat going to show the character of the man, and strong evidence that he had once in his life kissed the far famed "blarney stone." General McConnell was a candidate for the state senate and attended the general muster at Sharon, as was the custom among all candidates for office at that day, and O'Harra was there, noisy and boisterous as was his way, selling sweet cider from a barrell, placed in the tail-end of his wagon. The general in passing along near O'Harra, in company with two or three friends, was hailed by old Ned, and invited to walk up and take a little cider. After partaking of cider from old Ned's tincups, the general, being a candidate, could not do any better than offer to pay for the same and handed old Ned a five dollar bill, expecting some change in return. Old Ned put the bill in his pocket, remarking: "Jist the change, gineral. We shall vote for you, gineral. Old Chartered Ned will see to it, gineral, that all our corner shall be till the election. Success attend ye, gineral. What spalpeen is it that is so main as to run fornents ye? We want his name, so as to make no mistake. We hope ye will be elected. Good day, gineral, good day. Jist the change, gineral."

General McConnell was elected, but what influence O'Harra's cider had upon the result is not known to this day.

Meigsville Township

No record of the first organization of this township can be found; but there is on file in the clerk's office a poll book of an election held in the township for two justices of the peace on the 12th day of October, 1819.

No mention is made at what point in the township this election was held, but it appears that the old pioneers did assemble somewhere, and proceeded to hold the election by selecting Samuel Murray, Wm. Laughery and Andrew Welch, judges, and Thomas Murray and Wm. Murray, clerks. Only 25 votes were cast at this first election held in the township for justices of the peace, viz: Andrew Blime, Samuel Murray, Wm. Laughery, Wm. Murray, John Taylor, Sr., Henry Nickels, Robert Welch 1st, Thos. Taylor, Joseph Kidd, Wm. Horner, Henry Hoover, John Jones, Wm. Perry, John D. Rutledge, John Murray, Joseph Kelly, Thos. Murray, Robert Welch 2nd, John Henry Taylor, John Hesket, David Welch, John Wilson, Andrew Welch, Samuel Wickham and Isaac Counsil.

On counting out the ballots, Henry Taylor received 10 votes, Isaac Counsil 10, Wm. Horner 15 and John D. Rutledge 15. Horner and Rutledge were declared elected and commissioned as such in due time.

There is nothing very interesting or startling in the pioneer history of Meigsville. To ascertain who were the prominent citizens in and about the first organization of this township, the records at hand are examined and consulted. It is ascertained that Meigsville made but slow progress in her settlement up to 1820, when an election was held therein for a justice of the peace, and only 22 votes were cast. John W. Taylor, receiving 11 of the 22, was declared elected. Again, in 1822, at an election for J. P., only 26 votes were given, and Robert Welch, 2nd, had 16 votes and was declared elected.

Not until 1825 were there any great accessions, by emigration, to the inhabitants of the township. In April of that year an election was held for justice of the peace, and 41 votes given, of which number Joseph Kelly received 24, defeating Robert Welch, 2nd, an incumbent of that office at the time. About this period, the most prominent and numerous families of the township were the Mummeys, Counsils, Pattersons, Welches, Taylors, Ballards, Heads, Morrisons, Berrys, Kidds, Heskets, Martins, Kellys, Rutledges, Horners, and others not now remembered. The most of them in the last 40 years have been superseded by others, have been broken up and scattered and only a few of the above named families are now residents of the township.

For a long time the settlements of this township were confined to the water courses. Meigs Creek in this township received the "Dye's Fork," which runs through and along its eastern border, and then the main creek, which runs across the township from its northern boundary, entering Center township at its southeast corner. Four Mile is a considerable branch of the main creek, so called from the fact that it enters the creek just four miles from its mouth. Dye's Fork is so named after Thomas Dye who, at a very early day, say 75 to 80 years ago, settled high up on this branch, in what is now called Brookfield township, Noble county, and at one time a part of Morgan county. Meigs Creek, which enters the Muskingum river in Center township, waters the township of Meigsville in nearly all its parts. It was called Meigs Creek after R. J. Meigs, the first governor of Ohio after its admission into the Union.

Upon Meigs Creek and its branches the land is good and very productive. It was several years after the first settlements upon the creek and its branches before the congress lands upon the ridges were looked after and taken up. These uplands were fine hunting ranges to the early settlers and they were not backward in enjoying the fine sport afforded, and the tardiness in entering and occupying these lands was probably one of the principal causes in retarding the settlement and growth of the township.

The emigrants into this township were principally from Virginia and Pennsylvania. In a later day the township received accessions by the coming in of the Hedges, Wellses, Foutses, Neeleys, Tavenners, Siglers, McCormicks, Israels, Hammonds, Browns, Vincents, Filkills, McCartys, Spencers, Gheens, Shaffers, with several families direct from Ireland. So that at this day the number, respectability and enterprise of its people will well compare with any other community in the county.

This township was known at a very early date. In 1805 Robert McConnell and a party prospecting thru the woods of Meigsville, in the course of their journeyings in the wilderness, camped one night upon Four Mile Run at a prominent point now known as "Cave Rock," upon the lands of John Harmon, and near to Mr. Elliott's. At that period wolves were plenty, and the travelers were entertained during the night with their howling and impudence—with the prowling bear and the supple panther in the vicinity awaiting the spoils of the camp. Robert McConnell, before his departure in the morning, then and there (68 years ago) wrote his name, in a bold hand, upon the side of a smooth rock, with a piece of red chalk picked up in the run nearby, which sign-manual of the old pioneer might have been seen not long since by the inquisitive visitor.

In 1823 and up to 1825, in addition to the above list given for 1819, upon the record appear the names of the following early settlers: John Dickson, John Hughes, James Patterson, Thos. McCoid, Zephemiah Tyson, Alexander and James Boller, Louis Ramey, Christopher Mummey, Ebenezer Barkhurst, Josiah Kennison, Simon Elliott, Wm. Patterson, David Welch, Nicholas Durbin, Harrison Nichols, Samuel Fouts, Samuel Darnell, John Patterson, Samuel Farrell, John Duffey, Thomas Hopper, Samuel Morrison, Wm. Durbin, Andrew Welch, Robert Martin, Levi McCarty, and Robert Brown.

Of the last above list of Meigsville pioneers Mr. James Patterson is the only one known to be living, and he still resides at the place where he first located 50 or more years ago.

In the last above list of early settlers of Meigsville will be noticed the name of John Duffy. John was by birth an Irishman, possessing all the shrewdness and ready wit of that people. He was accustomed to freely mingle at all gatherings of the people, and never backward in taking a conspicuous part in the broils and fights that would sometimes spring up even among the best of the then inhabitants of Meigsville. John was an attentive visitor upon our early courts, either as a suitor, witness or spectator.

On one occasion he was called to the stand as a witness, and after he had been thoroughly examined as to what he knew touching the case, he was handed over, for cross examination, to Gen. Goddard, attorney for the opposite party. Gen. Goddard was then a young man, with considerable practice in our court, and as an attorney was quite popular and generally successful. He took Duffy in charge and plied him with all legal questions possible, to elicit something favorable to his client, or have John cross himself in his testimony in chief. In this undertaking he seemed to have failed and was about to give up and order his departure from the stand, when it occurred to the attorney to ask Duffy another question: "Well, Mr. Duffy, you have told us all about what he said about Taylor, Lupardis, and others, will you please tell us what he said about me?" "Is it what he said about you, Mr. Goddard, is it what you want to know? Well, Mr. Goddard, he said you was the damnedest rascal he ever had anything to do with, and I think he was about half right." 'Take your seat, Mr. Duffy," was the gruff order of Goddard. The whole audience was convulsed with uproarious laughter, while a smile might be perceived upon the visages of the bench of dignified judges.

Deerfield Township

In the early history of Morgan county, Deerfield, on her part, fails to make a long or interesting chapter. No record of the organization of the township is found, but it appears by a poll book on file in the clerk's office that on Feb. 5, 1820, an election was held at the house of Mr. Joshua Breeze for the purpose of filling a vacancy occasioned by the resignation of Wm. Massey. How and when Mr. Massey became a justice of that township no record can be found to explain the fact. The judges of this election were John Shutt, Wm. McKitrick and Josiah Wright; the clerks, Samuel Aikin and Jeremiah Weston. McKitrick and Weston were afterwards struck off into the new township of Union. The number of votes cast at this election foots up to forty, and the following named pioneers appeared and cast their ballots: John Tanner, Shubel Russell, John Hull, James Beldean, Reuben Porter, James Reed, Aaron Hainsworth, Isaac Whitaker, Andrew Grubb, Jonathan Norton, Silas Sailor, Philip Sailor, John Risen, Wm. Oliver, Lancet Oliver, George Pidcock, Josiah Joslin, Solomon Walker, James Murphy, Riley Joslin, John Morris, Martin Michael, Wm. Nixon, Samuel Buckley, Joshua Breeze, John Sniff, Wm. Joslin, Robt. Aikin, Patten Pherson, Hugh Riley, Joseph Pettet, Josiah Wright, Jeremiah Weston, Andrew Scott, John Shutt, Samuel Allard, and John Price.

It is supposed the above is a pretty full list of the adult male pioneers of the township at that period. There may be some few omissions, but their names do not at present come to our recollection. At this election, John Price received 31 votes, Wm. McKitrick 4, Elijah Ball 3, and John Morris and Samuel Aikin one vote each. Of this list of 40 pioneers, Silas Sailor, now a resident of Penn township, and Samuel Allard, now a resident of Homer township, are the only persons known to be living.

In the next year, 1821, at an election for justice of the peace, when Samuel Stanbery was elected, there appeared old pioneers, in addition to the above list, Joseph Edwards, Thos. Campbell, Enoch Winchell, Samuel Stanbery, Levi Lightie, Samuel Walker, Jonathan Edgington, Thomas Parks and Hugh Nixon.

At the regular spring election in 1823, for a J. P., there appeared, in addition to the above lists, the following named persons, who may properly be placed among the pioneers of Deerfield: Robert Stanbery, Alex. Brown, Andrew Grubb, John Hainsworth, Reason Ball, Foster Edwards, Joab Jones, Jonathan Adams, Wm. Atkins, Morgan O. Leary, Joseph Allard, Vatchel Ogg, John Lightie, John Briggs, John G. Wright, John Hollingshead, John Hopkins, Joshua Dicas, James Nelson, and Thomas Pettit. This election was set aside for the reason that John Price, a candidate and who received a majority of the votes cast, was one of the judges of the election.

In May, 1823, the election was run over, when John Price was reelected a J. P. There appeared at this election the following additional persons: John Campsey, Jacob Tedro, Elijah Atkins, and James Crawford.

Perhaps there is no township in the county producing less changes in its original proprietors than that of Deerfield. Where the old pioneers originally fixed themsleves, there the most of them sojourned until removed by death. This is in part accounted for from the fact that its soil is not quite so inviting to the enterprising agriculturists as that of other townships—yet its soil is durable and in some parts quite productive.

This township in the course of the last fifty years, has brought forth quite a number of gifted men who in the professions, in the various businesses and enterprises of the country, have become prominent. In laws, gospels and physics, her sons are somewhat prominent, and some of them hold high positions in their professions in their several localities.

She has sent forth a troop of active, energetic business men, scattered here and there throughout the land. Deerfield may well be proud of the position she holds, and if her soils do not prove as productive to the wants of man as other parts of the county, she has not been derelict in the production of men who, in the active turmoils and labors of life, have shown themselves well able to play their parts to admiration.

Penn Township

Penn township in its career is something like Deerfield, it has not made much history. There it stands, and through a series of 55 years will show a record for peace, thrift and morals, perhaps equal to the average townships of the county.

Its people at a very early day desiring to participate in the manifold blessings afforded by a local government, petitioned the county commissioners to be struck off into a new township. The new township was called Penn, taking its name from the illustrious founder of the great Commonwealth of Pennsylvania, that name being suggested as appropriate, from the fact that the neighborhood was then being fast filled up and settled by the followers of that renowned Quaker.

The Court of Common Pleas being duly informed of the fact, that the new township of Penn had been created, on the 7th day of July, 1819, with a bench of Associate Judges, directed their clerk to make upon the Journal the following order:—

"Whereas, it appears that our Commissioners of Morgan county, have set off a new township, by the name of Penn, ordered that said township be entitled to two Justices of the Peace; and that the qualified voters of said township be authorized to assemble at the house of John Harris in said township, on Saturday, the 24th inst, for the purpose of electing one or more Justices for said township."

Accordingly, on the said 24th day of July, A. D. 1819, the pioneer voters then of Penn, to the number of 29 assembled at the place designated in the above order, and then and there organized themselves for the purpose of electing one Justice of the Peace. It will be observed that Penn was authorized to "elect one or more justices for said township," yet after these pioneers had met, and not being so greedy for office at that day as is now manifest, they thought best not to elect two Justices as they were authorized to do by the order of the Court, but for the present to content themselves with one, as the state of society existing at that time did not require more than one Justice's Court.

Here follows a list of those who, on that day appeared and voted:—David Winnor, Sr., and Jr., Sam'l, Howard, William, Abner and John Widger, James McLain, Samuel King, Robert Todd, Isaac Davis, Joseph Mills, Thomas Nash, Ashet Tompkins, Joseph King, James Harris, John Simpson, Thomas Ackerson, Michel King, Wm. Hawkins, Richard Stileas, Samuel Work, John Harris, Jacob Hummell, James Ackerson, Abel Gilbert, Chas. Harward, Nathan Sidwell, John and Nathan Sidwell, Jr. Michael King, James Harris and Thomas Nash acted as judges, and Samuel King and Chas. Howard, as Clerks, of this election.

Charles Howard having received 27 of the 29 votes given, was declared elected. All of this number of pioneers, above named, are dead, except James McLain, who now resides in Homer township in this county. John Simpson, the next longest lived of the list, died a few months since, full of years and deservedly respected by all who enjoyed his acquaintance.

This township was generally settled by persons attached to the society of Friends or Quakers, most of them emigrating from Belmont and Jefferson counties, Ohio. This religious denomination built a meeting house near the village of Pennsville, which still stands and is regularly occupied as a prominent place of worship. This meeting house is perhaps the first and oldest church edifice in the county. Pennsville is the only village in the township. Nathan Sidwell, proprietor, had it surveyed and laid out into streets, alleys and lots in 1828.

The first settlements made in this township were upon Wolf Creek, which runs through a part of its territory. The lands upon this creek are of excellent quality and much desired by agriculturists as being well adapted to the production of cereals and grasses. The uplands of Penn with proper tillage and attention which for the last quarter of a century they have been receiving, have proved very productive in all the fruits, grains, grasses and vegetables, common to this climate and the soil.

At a very early day might be found settled along the bottoms of Wolf Creek such old pioneers as James McLain, Sr. and Jr., Isaac Davis, James, Warren and John Harris, Jacob Hummell, Jonathan Pierpoint, Abel King, and some others.

Out among the hills in other parts of the township, in addition to those named in the above list of voters, might be found James Campbell, Benjamin Jennings, John White, John Shaw, Samuel Smith, James Grubb, Anthony Hambel, Nimrod Williams, Casper Strahl, John Plummer, Samuel Embree, Isaac Clendenin, and in 1825, Joseph Barclay, John Rusk, Jesse Howard, Alexander and Marvin Gifford, William and Richard McPeak, Wells White, John R. Collins, John Baker and Zachariah Nash, appear upon the record, participating in the public affairs of the township. Most of these were settlers before the date of 1825.

The readers will notice among the voters at the first election, the name of William Hawkins, who afterwards became a prominent and leading citizen of the county and who served with credit the people of Morgan in several high and responsible stations. Here in Penn township, fifty years ago, Colonel Hawkins, then a young man, made his first appearance in the county, hiring himself out as a laboring hand to work at the business of chopping trees and clearing land. This pent up Utica was too contracted for a young man of the colonel's ambition and native ability; he therefore left the wilds of Penn township and located in McConnelsville at an early day, where he continued to reside, engaged in various enterprises, until a few years since when he died at an advanced age, much lamented.

Union Township

History informs us that Rhode Island was the last of the old thirteen states to come into the Federal Union; so Union township was the last township created to make a part of the confederated townships forming the new county of Morgan. This township was not set off until in October, 1821. Its territory, in fact, up to this period, was a howling wilderness. No white man, except a few trappers and hunters, lived in this territory beyond Wolf Creek.

A few pioneer inhabitants lived in and about the present neighborhood of Morganville and along the borders of Wolf Creek below. These first settlers generally went up into Deerfield to vote, and so continued until Union township was set off. An examination of the list of the voters who attended the first election in Union township will show who used to vote in Deerfield. At the October term of the court, and on the 30th of October, 1821, the court made the following order in regard to the new township of Union:

"Whereas: It appears that a new township, by the name of Union, has been created by the auditor of Morgan county; ordered that said township be entitled to two justices of the peace, and that the electors of said township meet at the house of Garrett Caviner, in said township, on the first Monday of December and proceed to elect two justices of the peace for said township."

Thereupon, on the 3rd day of December, 1821, the pioneer voters of the township convened as authorized at the house of Garrett Caviner, and proceeded to organize and hold the election for the two justices. Lazarus Pierce, Wm. Corner and Andrew Scott acted as judges; Geo. L. Corner and Wm. Scott as clerks. Nineteen pioneers cast their vote at this election, viz: Tobias Beckwith, James Scott, Nathan Green, George Nulton, Wm. Scott, David Scott, Wm. McKitrick, Geo. L. Corner, Daniel Viall, Robert Hainsworth, Wm. Corner, Andrew Scott, Lazarus Pierce, Saml. Stewart, John Chappellier, Garrett Cavinger, James Prosser, Wm. Lawrence, and Archibald Scott. The result of this election was that John Chappellier had 19 votes, Andrew Scott 11 and Wm. Corner 8.

The legality of this election was contested and tried before Wm. Massey, Joab Jones and Silvanus Piper, three freeholders of the county, who, in their report, say: "That from the testimony produced to us, do consider the said election illegal and of none effect."

This was rather a bad beginning for the pioneers of Union, showing that ignorance of the law existed even in that day. One of the causes of contest was that two of the candidates acted as judges of the election, viz: Corner and Scott. Another election was ordered and held Feb. 2, 1822, at which only 24 pioneers appeared. The new pioneer voters appearing at this election were Robert Love, John Bradley, Philip Warner, Thos. Rodman, Absolem Broderick, and Wm. A. Chappellier. John A. Chappellier and Wm. Corner were elected and commissioned. On July 9th, 1822, at an election for a justice of the peace, only 12 votes were cast. The additional pioneer voters were George Pierce, Jacob Spunge, John Quigley, James Chappellier and John Turner. George L. Corner, receiving all the votes, was declared elected.

It was not until about 1825 that Union made a start in the way of increasing her population. Up to that period the settlements were confined to Wolf Creek and some little upon Sunday Creek. About this time commenced a considerable emigration into the township from southeastern Ohio, Belmont county furnishing the most of them; and the settlement of several Irish families upon the waters of Upper Wolf and Sunday Creeks. At about this time appeared the Williamses, Glasses, Parsonses, Davises, Mastersons, Walpoles, Pughs, Barkhursts, and several other families. Many of their children still live in the township, and some of them are occupying the old homesteads of the early settlers. For many years the greater portion of the territory of Union was an unbroken and undisturbed forest, the resore of hunters and trappers. Particularly was this the case upon the waters of Sunday Creek. In these wild forests it was that such old hunters as the Hugheses, Wards, Loves, and Priests, carried on unmolested for years the hunting and trapping of the bear, wolf, deer, turkey, and other game.

The general character of the soil of the township is of the very best of limestone, durable and lasting, tho broken into ridges and valleys. Union township soil is perhaps the best in the county for all agricultural purposes. It is quite hilly off the creek bottoms, but is well watered by branches of Wolf and Sunday Creeks. It is now out of the woods in a measure, teeming with an industrious, enterprising and thrifty population. Wolf Creek, with its numerous branches, drains a large scope of territory in the counties of Washington and Morgan, and with one of its branches, runs through Union township, finding its head springs in Deerfield township.

This creek derives its name from the great number of wolves found among the hills at an early day by the pioneer trappers, who visited and frequented its waters for that express purpose. Sunday Creek, a branch of the Hocking river, has some of its head springs in Union township, and one of its branches runs through its southwestern border. The name of Sunday was given to this creek by the early government surveyors who, in running one of the range lines, pitched their camp upon this creek on Sunday. The next day, in the progress of their work, they camped upon a creek further north and gave it the name of Monday, and thus finishing their line in that direction, they had no further use for the days of the week in naming creeks.

This township being the latest settled territory in the county, and being somewhat out of the way of early emigration, it became somewhat infested by a few outlaws, who had their haunts and made their rendezvous upon the waters of Sunday Creek, a terror and the common talk in all the borders. Their operation in the way of stealing horses was extensive and carried on for some years, and was not entirely broken up until after the settlements became too dense for their safety and the success of their frequent forays upon distant parts of the country, and, in fact, not until after the indefatigable efforts made against them by the late Wm. Ramsey, Esq., prosecuting attorney of Morgan county, seconded by the law officers of Perry and Athens counties.

For a long time was Sunday Creek known as "Horse Thief Valley," and a lost horse from any part of the state might be traced and found somewhere upon the waters of Sunday Creek, either in the counties of Athens, Perry, or Morgan. Several interesting incidents of the way and manner in which this horse stealing business was carried on for years might be related, and the exploits of the principal actors in these scenes might in their relation be made interesting to the present and coming generations. All the actors of these horse-jockeying exploits have become dispersed or have "gone to that bourne from whence no traveler ever returns," leaving behind them a history in no way enviable or worthy of imitation.

The township has entirely outlived the bad name once possessed, and the places upon Sunday Creek that once knew these outlaws are now held and occupied by an entirely different population and by men who are engaged in entirely different pursuits.

Windsor Township

Windsor township was organized like the other new townships of the county The county commissioners set it off by bounds, and the court, at their July term, and on the 7th day of July, 1819, made the following order in regard to this township:

"Whereas, it appears to the court that our commissioners of Morgan county have erected a new township by the name of Windsor; ordered, that the township be entitled to two justices of the peace; and that the qualified electors of said township be authorized to assemble at the house of John Lucas, in said township, on Saturday, the 24th instant, for the purpose of electing two justices of the peace for said township of Windsor."

In compliance with the above order the pioneer voters of the township met on the 24th day of July, 1819, and organized themselves into a town meeting and proceeded with the election. The first thing they did was to appoint Richard Cheadle, Silvanus Newton and Silvanus Olney, judges, and Ephraim Wight and Samuel M. Dike the clerks to conduct the election.

The number of pioneers turning out and voting at this election numbered 44, and is believed to be a full list of the adult males of the township at that day. The following embrace the names of these pioneers first appearing in the organization of their township: John Craft, Isaac Melvin, Joseph Cheadle, Lyman Sherman, Samuel Stacy, John Mathany, Nathaniel Lucas, Joseph Widger, John Cheadle, Levi Davis, Nathaniel Eveland, Samuel Johnson, Levi Ellis, Samuel Henry, Franklin Hersey, Wm. Davis, 1st, Wm. Henry, Thomas Davis, Adelphia Webster, Luther Dearborn, Silvanus Olney, Nicholas Coburn, Padock Cheadle, David Emerson, Frederick Eveland, John Cheadle, Jr., Prince Godfrey, Samuel M. Dike, Alfred Ellis, Ephrim Ellis, Wm. Davis, 2nd, Elisha Hand, Daniel Dennis, Silvanus Newton, Ephraim Ellis, Asa Emerson, Jr., Ephraim Wight, Joseph Morris, Richard Cheadle, Michael Devin, Barzilla Coburn, Nathan Dearborn, Barney Sutliff, and Samuel Dennis.

At this election, Isaac Melvin received 29 votes, Adelphia Webster 39, Levi Ellis 14, Samuel White, Richard Cheadle and Ephraim Wight one vote each. Melvin and Webster were by the usual proclamation declared the expounders of law and the dispensers of justice for the next three years within the bailiwick of the new township of Windsor. Only one of these 44 pioneers whose names are recorded above is now living, Mr. Levi Ellis, now of Marion township, and, in fact, but few of their progeny are to be found within the bounds of the township where their ancestors once ruled and had control of affairs. They are (the children) either dead or gone west, and but few are found upon Big Bottom.

At an election held for a justice of the peace in December following when Levi Ellis was elected, Andrew Dennis, Ephraim C. Ellis and Isaac Ellis appear in addition to the above list. Mr. Isaac Ellis, only, survives, at a good old age, and is still a resident of the township.

At an election held in January, 1821, for J. P., when Wm. Davis was elected, Silas B. Hinman, Thos. Davis, Israel Davis, Hannarriel Newton, Joshua Davis, Oman Olney, and John B. Perry enrolled their names upon the public records for the first time.

In July, 1822, when Adelphia Webster was reelected J. P., Wm. Patterson and Jacob Dewitt appear as early settlers. In December, 1823, fifty years ago, when Wm. Davis was reelected a J. P., the following named pioneers made their appearance and cast their votes: Jeremiah Spurgeon, Ridgway Craft, Wm. Rannells, Thomas Atkinson, John R. Porter, Wm. Lucas, Thomas Tufts, Jesse Craft, John Eveland, Thomas Walker, Arnold Lippett, Timothy Blackmore, Samuel Craigg, Richmond Cheadle, Olcutt White, and Elijah Smith. Of all this list of 72 pioneers of Windsor, who had a settlement or an abiding place within its borders, 50 or more years ago, only Levi and Isaac Ellis named above are recognized as now living.

It has been suggested that in those early days several of the pioneer settlers were boatmen, engaged in the business of propelling the keel boats from Zanesville to Pittsburg and the Kanawha salt works, that being the case, their names do not appear upon the records consulted.

The first settlers of Windsor township were emigrants from the New England states, and they brought with them many of the usages, customs and ways of that people; and as far as practicable were observed here among themselves, in the wilds upon the Muskingum.

For some years after the organization of the township it was the practice to hold their town meetings on the first Monday in April, the day designated by law, and select their township officers. These elections were held with as little delay as possible and the result duly announced. On the occasion of such an election, when all the voters of the township who intended to take part in the same were supposed to be present, proclamation was made for what office they were called upon first to fill, and for the voters to come forward and manifest their wishes. If it was the township clerk they were to elect, a crier would proclaim: "Prepare to vote for a clerk." The ballots were then received by a teller in a hat or a box and when all had voted the announcement was made: "Polls closed for clerk."

The ballots were counted and the result duly announced. The crier would then declare "The polls turned, prepare to vote for a constable." In like manner the voters went thru the same process adopted in the election of clerk and constable of a long list of elective officers: Three trustees, number of supervisors, three overseers of the poor, three fence viewers, treasurer, lister, and some other township officers then unknown to the law but thought necessary in the then present state of society, were thus elected and proclaimed. This way of electing township officers was followed up to about 1830, when some new comers settling among them, innovated in this business, and demanded that the mode of conducting elections should be changed and the statute should be complied with. This mode of holding elections may seem strange to the present day people, but it was fair and freely acquiesced in by the old settlers, beside it was expeditious and, if not altogether legal, it was devoid of errors.

Windsor township will be found bountiful in its early reminiscences which cannot now be noted. Already in these chapters is found a place for a full account of the Big Bottom massacre, by the savages, in 1790, and also the exploits and mysterious killing of the old Shawnee chief, "Silverheels," both important historical events connected with the first settlement of the township.

For many years the locations and settlements were confined to the rich, productive bottom lands along the Muskingum river; but few ventured out into the hills, as the soil was not so inviting and desirable as that upon the river. The uplands were entirely allotted to hunting and for some distance on each side of the river the territory for many years was thus occupied. The "circular hunt," causing rare sport and much spoils, was quite common among the early settlers. At these hunts all turned out with their dogs and guns, and in the closing in of the circle, there would be found in the area many deer, turkeys and much small game, now and then the sheep-killing wolf, against which the early pioneer was always at war, would turn up. Sometimes the bear, the panther, the wildcat and the fox would become easy prey to the rifles of the sturdy woodsman, or lively and interesting sport to the young men, boys and dogs. These kinds of sports continued for a long time, until one of the hunters present at one of these sports was accidentally shot and killed by another, which forever after put an end to that kind of pastimes among the early settlers of Windsor.

The openings and improvements at first were limited in extent. The pioneer settler in his efforts in this direction was content to make a home with a sufficient cleared soil to sustain himself and family for the time being,—two or three acres of corn, with a truck patch planted by the settler, whose ideas at that day of enterprise, energy and improvement did not extend much beyond the log cabin, the small area of cultivated territory, his corn meal, hog and hominy and some few other necessaries—powder and lead, fish hooks, etc. In this undertaking he, however, bestowed much labor in subduing the great growth of timber, standing and incumbering the ground in every direction, with interminable and almost impenetrable thickets of undergrowth all over the land. The Big Bottom pioneers and all the early settlers along the river made haste to plant out orchards, after the examples set them by the early settlers about the Waterford, Marietta and Belpre settlements, so that forty years ago there could be found in this township apples, peaches, and cherries in great abundance. Some of the apples were of the very best varieties, and are still equal to the more modern.

The products of these orchards, in the fall of the year, found a market at Zanesville and the few intermediate salt works, in exchange for salt. Apples and cherries in great abundance were carried up the river in open canoes, in pirogues, propelled against the stream by the setting pole in the hands of experienced watermen.

In those early days they had no roads worthy the name, and blazed bridle paths along the banks of the river through the interior would suffice for their present wants, and were about the extent of the improvements that the township could then boast of. The river was their only channel of communication and commerce; the rough dugout, the light canoe, the huge pirogue and the keel boat were their only water craft, in which the traveling and trade were conducted and which were considered a very cheap but somwhat laborious mode of transportation and intercourse. Now are no longer to be seen upon our waters those primitive craft; they, like the birchbark canoe of the Indian, have long since disappeared, and in their places, for the purposes for which they were so convenient and handy, is found the steamboat of all models and sizes; tolerably good roads penetrating all parts of the township, with numerous and quite a variety of fine road vehicles make easy and expeditious the passage to trade and travel all over, in, and through the township.

Windsor township, up to the inauguration of the improvement of the Muskingum river, continued unpretending, and without any considerable improvements in farms, buildings, etc. The inhabitants seemed content to live as they had always lived, free, independent and not troubling themselves very much in the ways of progress going on in other parts of the county.

The river improvement, in time, produced an almost complete and entire change in the occupiers of the soil, in the appearance of the farms and buildings, and in the energy, enterprise and thrift of the people. This improvement seemed to be an elevating power, giving to its people new life and enterprise, and inviting within its borders men of means and energy. There may yet be found a few, and but very few, of those first settlers and owners of the soil and their children within its territory. Now and then an old mansion house, dilapidated and tottering with age, may be found upon the river banks, built and once occupied by an early settler. They and their children have removed, and those old landmarks, once conspicuous to the river traveler and familiar to the early boatmen, have given away to other occupiers and much better structures.

Coming down to 1832, we find that Nathan Sidwell, Jr., laid out on the west bank of the river the village of Windsor; in 1833 the Beswicks and Joseph McMahan laid out an addition, and in 1839 G. W. Sanburn laid out an adjoining village, and named it Stockport, and from appearance is one village. This is the only village in the township, enjoying considerable trade with the interior and through its enterprising people put forth at times during its existence it has become a place of considerable business, trade and commerce.

York Township

The County Commissioners having set off the new township of York, the court at their July session in 1819 (July 7th), made the following order in regard to York:

"Whereas, it appears the commissioners of our county of Morgan have set off a new township by the name of York; ordered that said township be entitled to two justices of the peace, and that the qualified electors of said township be authorized to assemble at the house of John Stoneburner on Saturday, the 24th instant."

In pursuance to the command of this order the old pioneer settlers of York met at the house of John Stoneburner to put into execution this order. They selected William Atkins, James McAdoo and Henry Smith to act as judges, and Elijah Atkins and Jacob Ebert as clerks of the election. At this election there were cast 30 votes, which no doubt was a pretty full list of the settlers of York at that day, 55 years ago. Below follow the names of the voters at this election:

Levi Deaver, James McAdoo, Elijah Atkins, Henry Smith, William Atkins, Bartholomew Longstreth, Christian Shirk, Samuel Rogers, Jas. Dikus, George Smith, Peter Burgoon, Benjamin Parker, Samuel Pletcher, John Shultz, Peter Stoneburner, Henry Weller, John Stoneburner, Chas. Stoneburner, Robert Rose, William Foreaker, Richard Burgoon, Joshua Foreaker, Michael George, Sr., Patrick Ryan, Michael George, Jr., James Longstreth, Cornelius Ferrell, Chas. Burgoon, Luther Wilson, and Jacob Ebert. Not one of the above list is known to be living. Michael George and Peter Burgoon each received 28 votes and were declared elected; and Jacob Ebert, three votes. It will be observed that this poll of this election shows one more ticket in the box than there were voters. This was either an error of the officers of the election, or someone voted two votes for Ebert. It shows that 55 years ago frauds were committed at elections, or errors were made unobserved. No doubt it was an error of the clerks in the counting and scoring, for in those days the honest pioneers of York would have scorned the perpetration of an election fraud.

At an election held April 2nd, 1821, when Christian Shirk was elected a J. P., the following other early settlers appear to have had an abiding place in York, viz: Jeremiah Wise, Thomas Coleman, Henry Pletcher, Barnet Hampshire, Jacob Swope, James Burgoon, and John Herron.

Coming down to an election held in the township in Oct., 1824, when Wm. Large was elected a J. P., the following additional pioneers made their appearance for the first time and took part in the affairs of the township, viz: Stephen Foreaker, Shadrick Allard, Nathan Moody, Solomon Brown, William Delaney, William Foraker, Jr., Thomas Foreaker, Jr., Peter Thomas, Charles Bond, John Dodds, John McIntire, Reuben Allard, George Shaffer, Philip Stout, Nicholas Swingle, William Large, Amos Conaway, Thomas Foreaker, Sr., Samuel Allard, Edward Sowers, Jonathan Walls, Casper Trout, Jacob Torn, John Smith, Jas. W. Moody.

Upon the list of voters in July, 1825, the following additional names may properly be published as old settlers in York, viz: George Houpt, John George, James Coho, John Geiger, Jacob Sowder and Samuel Bagley.

There is nothing in the early history of York township deserving particular notice at this time. As the object of the present writing is to obtain from reliable sources for preservation and future reference the names of the adult pioneers of the township in and about the period of 50 years ago and at the time (1819) when they first organized themselves into a political community.

The great body of the first settlers of York township were Pennsylvania Dutch. Some years afterwards there was a considerable emigration direct from Germany into the township, so that the larger portion of the inhabitants at the present period are either German or their descendants.

The general soil of this township is not of the very best quality, but by the manner in which it is managed by its thrifty and industrious people, the land is made to produce exceedingly well in all the agricultural products common to this part of Ohio.

Deavertown is a considerable village, located in the west part of the township, laid out in 1815 by Levi Deaver, who was its proprietor and who has been deceased these many years. It is the oldest town in the county and, if we rightly remember, was first called New Market.

Morgan Township

When and in what manner Morgan township was organized and obtained a political existence is not known to the oldest inhabitant, nor is there any very clear record of the fact extant. It was an original surveyed township, five and six miles in extent, in range 12 (that range being only five miles wide). All that part of Malta township within range 12 and including section 29 of the original township, in 1819 was a part of the then Morgan township, of which we now write about. The county commissioners, in 1819, in creating the new township of Penn, struck off from the south side of Morgan five sections and then took a like number of sections from the south side of Bloom, and annexed them to Morgan. This is about the extent of our information in regard to the creation of Morgan township.

In the early part of 1819 we find only a partial organization of the township existing. James Young was the only acting justice of the peace in the township, and when or how he became such we have no knowledge. He had his office in an old, leaky, dilapidated shed attached to his dwelling on lot No. 64, corner of Main and Union streets, McConnelsville, where he dispensed justice and attended to the legal wants of his neighbors with dignity and dispatch unsurpassed by any one of his numerous successors. Esquire Young was a molder and brick mason, and built the first brick dwelling in the county for Jacob Adams, who now occupies the same, in a good state of preservation, as the "Adams House" on the southwest side of the public square. He also made the brick and put up the first court house in the county. Young being almost constantly occupied in his mechanical pursuits and, besides, a tavern keeper, his court days, from necessity, were held on Saturdays; on which occasions much legal business was transacted and disposed of in a way peculiar to those early days.

Legal business accumulating in the township, it was deemed necessary to have another justice's court opened. Thereupon, the trustees of the township, in the absence of any action on the part of the common pleas court, ordered an election to be held on the 31st day of July, 1819, to elect an additional justice of the peace.

The first political demonstration we have any account of among the early settlers of the township was the election thus ordered and held in the town of McConnelsville on the 31st day of July, 1819. Alexander McConnell, Daniel Chandler and John Pettit, judges; Jesse L. Paschal and Simon Pool, Jr., clerks of election. In a former chapter of these reminiscences will be found a pretty full account of this, the first election held in the township. We now refer to the poll book of that election to obtain a list of the pioneers on that day.

They were Louis Ramsey, Gilbert Olney, Nathaniel Sprague, Wm. M. Dawes, Amasa Piper, Simeon Pool, John Bell, Alexander McConnell, Simeon Pool, Jr., Jacob Adams, Joseph Wyatt, Wm. Lewis, Silvanus Piper, Jacob R. Price, John Petit, Robt. Aikne, Jr., John Smith, Wm. Hughes, John Williams, Philip Kahler, John Seaman, Abraham Hughes, Benjamin T. Johnson, Isaac Walbridge, Timothy M. Gates, Wm. C. Johnson, Israel Redman, Jonathan McMullen, Wm. Murphy, James Larrison, Nathaniel Shepard, James Young, Saml. A. Barker, Jonas Fox, Charles Brian, and Henry Awmiller —numbering 36 pioneers. Daniel Chandler, a judge, and Jesse L. Paschal, a clerk of election, did not vote, making the number 38. Eleven of this list resided within the present corporate limits of McConnelsville—all others resided in the county and the most of them on the Malta side of the township. At this election, Timothy M. Gates was elected, receiving 15 votes of the 36. Of this list of 36 pioneers voting at this election, Jacob Adams is the only survivor. Charles Brian, whose name occurs in this list, recently died at his residence in this village.

On the 22nd day of January, 1820, an election was held for a justice of the peace, at which Timothy M. Gates, Gilbert Olney and Alexander McConnell acted as judges, and John Seaman and Jacob R. Price as clerks. The following pioneers for the first time appear upon the records, viz.: Wm. B. Young, Moses Lawrence, John Davis, Joseph Smith, William Brown, David Smith, Theophelius Caton, Isaac Miles, Samuel H. Gates, Henry Snider, John Jack, Jonathan Porter, Simeon Murgardidge, William Palmer and Jacob P. Springer. Isaac Walbridge of the village of Malta was elected, receiving 24 votes out of 31 given. The larger portion of these pioneers were residents of the village and township in April, 1819.

In this list of pioneers will be found the name of Isaac Miles. He was peculiar in his ways, blunt, decided and determined. Among his numerous friends and acquaintances he was known as Deacon Miles, not that he possessed any particular christian virtues appertaining to that kind of a church officer nor had he connection with any of the theological organizations extant among us at that early day, but from his peculiarities displayed on all occasions.

For some years he was one of the constables, and the law during his administration made it the duty of the constable to visit every newcomer settling in the township, and notify him or her to depart the same, so that he or she should not in any event become a public charge upon the township. This was called "warning out," and the notice in the hands of Constable Miles was given to everyone, no matter what might be their station or circumstances in life; the rich and the poor were sure to receive a call from Deacon Miles. Constable or Deacon Miles in his rounds of "warning out," came to the domicile of a lone widow, and without notice of his approach he bolted across the threshold of her cabin and in no smooth, pleasant or consoling voice blurted out, "Madam, I warn you out of the township and off the face of God's earth." The woman, surprised at the sudden intrusion of the officer of the law and his peremptory commands, raising her hands toward heaven, cried out, "My God, Mr. Miles, off the face of God's earth; where shall I go to?" "Go to," asks the Deacon, "go to the Kanawha salt works." The Kanawha salt works at that day was a sort of an asylum for the lame, halt and blind, and unfortunate, and also a refuge for those who were compelled to leave the country for the country's good. Deacon Miles many years ago departed this life, and no one at this day can point out his resting place.

In continuation of the pioneer list of Morgan township, the following additional pioneers first make their appearance upon the record at an election held June 3rd, 1,820, viz.: Thomas Byers, Robert Morgan, John Berry, Leonard St. Clair, Timothy Gaylord, William Van Horn, Charles Kinsel, Sr., John Kennison, Isaac Sprague, Jonathan Williams, Isaac Hedges, David Miller, George Miller, William Fouts, William Sprague, Swan Vance, Edwin Corner, John Scott, Robert Robinson, Joseph McConnell and David Irvin.

At this election Jacob Fouts was duly elected justice of the peace, receiving 22 votes; Jacob R. Price, 18, and Amasa Piper, 6. Five or six of the above named were residents of the township in the fore part of 1819.

Afterwards, on the 29th day of August, 1820, an election was held for J. P., at which election there were 46 votes cast, and the additional pioneers participating in the local political strife were: Alex Brown, John Lawson, Jonathan Whitney, John Lucas, Fras. Lucas, Obediah Scott, Barney Scott, Robert Henery, Wm. Spurgeon and Robert Winter. At this election Timothy Gaylord received 27 votes and Alexander McConnell, 19. Thomas Byers, an elector, contested the legality of this election before Simon Merwin, Thos. Devin and John White, freeholders of the county. The election was declared legal and Timothy Gaylord was duly commissioned. At that day the local party distinctions of Brimstones and Juntos prevailed, and all the local political contests were marked with much strife and bitter feeling. Gaylord was a Brimstone, and McConnell a Junto. Some account of these parties of Brimstones and Juntos, their rise and fall, will be found in a former chapter of these reminiscences.

An election for a J. P. was held on the 7th August, 1821, at which election 61 votes were cast. Francis A. Barker received 26 votes and Timothy M. Gates, 30. The election of Gates, who was the head-center of the Brimstone faction, was chronicled as a great victory for the Brimstones. The following pioneers for the first time appeared and have their names registered: Jesse Spurgeon, Lloyd Piatt, Martin Troby, Levi Ellis, Caleb Wells, Nathan Wilder, Daniel Chandler (Chandler was a judge of the first election but did not vote), John Clemens, Thos. Barr, Alex R. Pinkerton, Jacob Kahler, Stephen Gates, Sr., John B. Stone, Frederick Pope, John Patterson, Orange Walker, and John West.

On the 1st day of April, 1822, an election for a J. P. was held, and at which election 70 votes were cast, of which Jeremiah Stephens received 40 votes and Wm. Palmer, 30. This result was claimed as a Junto victory. The following named pioneers appeared for the first time, viz.: Wm. Hawkins, Edo Stubbs, George Newcomb, Wm. Stephens, Zenas Cox, John Patton, Allen Robinet, Jeremiah Conaway, Jeremiah Stephens, John Stutes, Micah Adams, Rufus P. Stone, William Dawes, and Isaac James. Some of them were residents of the township in 1819.

Fifty years ago on the 14th day of October (1823) an election for J. P. was held, at which election 89 votes were given, of which Alexander McConnell received 48 votes and Timothy Gaylord, 40. This was the last exciting local contest between Brimstones and Juntos, and was a triumph for the latter.

The presidential election coming on the next year (1824), the Brimstone and Junto partizans were, to some extent, lost in that memorable presidential strife. Breaking loose from former political associations, Brimstones and Juntos were found working harmoniously together for some one of the presidential candidates of the period. Politics then, as now, made strange bedfellows. McConnell and Gaylord, who 12 months before were engaged in a bitter strife over the office of justice of the peace, upon the Junto and Brimstone platforms, were in 1824 found together, shoulder to shoulder, striving for the election of Clay, and in 1828 were leading Jacksonians;

while others equally as bitter and hostile towards each other in the local political strifes of that day would embrace each other in a friendly hug in 1824, and then throw up their hat and strive for the election of Jackson or Adams. Then it was that the Brimstone and Junto factions commenced to die out and the most of their bitter partisans were lost in the national contest of 1824 and in that of 1828.

At this election the following additional pioneers made their appearance and were enrolled upon the record, viz.: W. C. Shugart, Amon Wells, John P. Ferrell, Samuel Morrison, Holmes Morrison, James Hughes, Wm. Wells, George Dawes, Charles Dawes, Ebenezer Hammel, Augustus Hoskin, Robt. P. Oliver, Benj. Beckwith, Jacob Slinger, Matthew Lutton, James Baker, Samuel Baker, George Newman, Michael Wiseman, Joel Olney, Silas Lorey, Thos. Dugan, Enoch Loper, William Brooks, James A. Gillespie, and Samuel Pollard.

The list of pioneers of Morgan township on the 14th day of October, 1823, and prior thereto, is here given, numbering 144. Several of these pioneers became residents of the township long before they made their appearance at the elections in which their names are mentioned, and no doubt some few names are omitted from the list who should have a place in the same for the reason that they did not attend these several elections and have themselves registered. To a great extent we have depended upon the poll books consulted for a full list, but we find the names of Rev. Geo. Russell, Joseph Barrow, John Collison, James Clemens, and some others, unnaturalized foreigners and early settlers whose names are omitted from the record before us.

Of this list of 144 names, the large majority of whom were sojourners and active men in the township 50 and more years ago, Isaac Hedges, George Newman, Jacob Adams, David Miller, William Fouts, Edwin Corner, John B. Stone, W. C. Shugart and Amon Wells are the only known survivors. Isaac Hedges, George Newman, Jacob Adams, John B. Stone and Amon Wells still reside in the county; Wm. Fouts emigrated to Oregon some years since and there resides; W. C. Shugart lives in Indiana; Edwin Corner in Franklin county, and David Miller in Muskingum county. Only nine of the 144 pioneers of Morgan township of 50 years ago can now answer to roll call; but many of their descendants still sojourn in the township and county.

In these early days of which we write about, there were among us some few old pioneers who could not well be classed under any common description of mankind; their like we shall perhaps never meet with again, who frequented our courts, and were about on public days, and who practiced more or less at the bars of our village taverns. At that day, besides the judges, lawyers, jurors, suitors and witnesses, a goodly number of spectators were in attendance to the proceedings of our early courts. Not only were they present to witness the court proceedings, but in those days, when newspapers were not as prodigal in their circulation as now, a class of persons would come out on such occasions to learn the current news of the period, and indulge themselves in the discussion and investigation of the events going on in the outside world, and have their friendly chats with one another upon various local subjects and questions then and there suggested. Fifty years ago but few newspapers found a circulation within the bounds of Morgan county; perhaps the two Zanesville papers and one or two weeklies from east of the mountains would be the extent of the circulation through two or three postoffices in the whole county, and those delivered by a weekly horseback mail. All inquiring and wide-awake men residing away from the county seat, contentedly living in their rude log cabins, upon new farms, generally depended for the news of the day on the now and then traveler, passing through the country who, for his supposed fund of news and gossip, was always a welcome guest, and hospitably entertained and kept out of bed to a late hour in the night answering the many questions of his inquisitive host, and also upon those neighbors who now and then emerged from the woods into the outside world who, on their return, would impart such information of what was going on. For these and other purposes might be found congregated at the county seat on court days all kinds of characters.

Among this motley and somewhat promiscuous throng of visitors might be seen Joseph D.—, an early settler of Muskingum county, residing close upon the borders of Bristol township. Old Joe D. was one of those men we sometimes meet with, possessing a "rough and unseemly exterior, but a good heart within."

He was of great courage and supreme daring; a successful hunter, who had in many contests vanquished the beasts of the forest, admirably well skilled in all the shifts, expedients and customs of the early settler, and was truly a hardy, active and accomplished backwoodsman. His native abilities were superior and without the advantages of school and book education, he was looked upon as a prodigy. He could, therefore, cheerfully accommodate himself without inconvenience or perplexity to all kinds of company he met with. Old Joe was there in all his native dignity and perfect equanimity of mind. It is remembered, on one occasion old Joe was hard put for lodgings; all the taverns in the village were crowded and an accommodation for old Joe could not be found. He had no place to rest his weaving body and befuddled head. At that day our village plat presented plenty of brush and log heaps; old Joe settled himself at a large log heap for the night's lodging, fired up the pile and, after the custom of the hunter, made his bed and sweetly reposed during the night unmolested. At early dawn old Joe made his appearance at the bar of the village tavern, thirsty, but somewhat refreshed in body. He called for his gill of Moxahala. At that day liquor was dealt out indiscriminately to all comers in measures of gallons, quarts, pints, half-pints, gills and half-gills, the customer calling for the quantity and the barkeeper promptly and publicly supplying the same, and no questions propounded. On this occasion it seemed that a full gill was sufficient for Joe's first morning libation. He readily and with expedition turned it off, and took his position among the throng of village loungers who had been indulging their early morning dram. One of those present seeming to know something about old Joe's whereabouts and how he had fared the night before, and thinking to have a little fun at old Joe's expense, began: "Well, well, Mr. D., if it is not impertinent on my part, I would like to know where you lodged last night."

"Well, sir," replied old Joe, "I do not take it as impertinent for one neighbor to interrogate another in regards to his whereabouts in this neck of the woods, particularly if his absence should be in the night season, for, you know, Mr. W.—, I am not much concerned about where I shall sleep, what I shall eat or how much I shall drink. Well, sir, I sojourned last night at the tavern with the sign of "God help us," without roof, side board, bed or bar."

"Well, Mr. D., whereabouts in town is the tavern located?"

Old Joe, stretching himself up to his full length, then over six feet, and in a sonorous and deliberate pronunciation, said: "Sir, that place of accommodation for the wayfarer will be found in this town on the corner of Poplar, Beech, Hickory and Walnut streets—with much hickory bark to light your way, but nothing to hostler or landlord to pay."

"Well, well, Mr. D., if your tavern occupies all these four corners it must be an extensive structure. I am done. Landlord, set out the drinks."

By this time the audience had increased to that extent that a quart or more was found necessary to go round, and it went round at the expense of the indiscreet inquisitor, and old Joe, in the midst of jingling glasses, much cheering and uproar, was unanimously voted the hero of the hour.

On another occasion, when in a sober circle of neighbors, someone was boasting of his recent religious conversion and under whose ministry the event had taken place. Old Joe patiently listened to the tale of the new convert and, being somewhat skeptical in such serious matters, bluntly broke out: "Yes, yes, my young friend, we read in the Good Book that in olden times one Balaam was converted by the braying of an ass—why not have the same miracle take place at this day, here on Meigs Creek? Yes, why not?"

McConnelsville 54 Years Ago

For some years after the War of 1812, a commendable military spirit existed among and pervaded our people. Still remembering the cruelties and outrages perpetrated by the British and their savage allies upon our defenseless frontiers in the late bloody contest with that ancient enemy of ours; remembering the unparalleled successes of our little navy upon the ocean and lakes against proud old England, who arrogantly claimed to be the mistress of the seas, and remembering the daring exploits of Brown, Ripley, Scott, Jackson, and a host of other heroes upon the land, made almost every man a soldier and tended to infuse into the mass of our people the idea of the necessity of preparing in time of peace for war when it should come. This military spirit and concern lingered among our people here in their new settlements down too about 1830, when from the want of encouragement and countenance of our legislators it entirely died out.

When the war with Mexico, in 1846, and the Rebellion, in 1861, came upon us, our people were found without any military organization, destitute of any discipline and without suitable war weapons in their hands. All deficiencies, however, in these emergencies, were soon supplied, and in a short time we made ourselves formidable in force, discipline and armament sufficient to stand against the world. We venture, here, to suggest that from past experience, there seems at this day to be no necessity for us to keep up a state militia or a standing army beyond local necessity and general defense. Hereafter it should be our policy to depend upon a small regular army and navy properly stationed and kept well disciplined, armed and equipped as a nucleus around which our volunteer citizen soldiery may rally to repel an invading foe or quell domestic trouble.

Then it was in those early days we had our general musters or parading of the state militia by companies and regiments. These were times of rare sport and fun for all participating, and everybody, their wives and their children, came to the show—though the officers put on military airs and tried to look severe of countenance and manners, and defiant, making believe that they were born to command; yet no one seemed to be frightened. The state militia was divided into companies, regiments, brigades and divisions.

Then the individual who was possessed of military aspirations might by election, not promotion, rise from the humble rank of a private to that of the highest military position; and at that day we were by no means deficient in material and pretensions out of which to make our officers. The major general of a division received his appointment and commission from the governor, and Gen. John Lidy of Somerset, Perry county, Ohio, was at one time the major general of this division of Ohio militia. Gen. Lidy but seldom made his appearance. He seemed to be contented to bear the honors of the place with dignity and at his own expense.

In the early settlement of the county the general musters were annually held and the "muster men" of the / county, between the ages of 18 and 45, were regularly enrolled and required to perform two days military duty each year, or subject to fines and penalties. In the very earliest days there was but one regiment in the county, and for some years it met for muster upon the farm of Joseph Devereaux on Mann's Fork of Meigs Creek, now occupied by Rufus Cotton, being the most central and suitable point. As the population of the county increased, a brigade was created, and other regiments were formed, with Alex McConnell the first brigadier general. After the creation of the brigade it was that our village was first honored by a general parade of the first regiment.

The first general muster in our village, about 800 strong, was formed in line upon Center street, with its right resting in front of E. Corner's tavern, where Adams & Kahler's store now stands, and marched hence for military exericse and drill into a stake and ridered stubble field situated to the north of Center street, including all the space from H. R. Pinkerton's corner east along Center street to the break of the hill, and ample space was here found for all the military maneuvers in vogue at that day, and for a full display of official military knowledge and dignity. In this stubble field, Col. ————, with his staff and the other field officers first appeared with his regiment for drill. Preparatory to the formation and parade of the regiment, companies were formed, ranked and sized, in different parts of the village. Each company supplied itself with a drum and fife, and kept up an interminable racket all day long and about those noisy musical instruments might be found congregated all the boys of the village and country, who in their youthful opinions estimated the drummer and fifer the greatest men in the regiment.

In these stirring, noisy times, all over town might be seen the sergeants of companies running to and fro, lustily calling for the privates to "fall in, fall in; all who belong to Capt. ———— company, fall in!" When the men of the company were gotten together, the captain would make his appearance, bedecked and bedizened in his military uniform, which in those primitive military days consisted of a faded cloth coat, with rows of brass buttons down the breast, a faded and rusty epaulet, and old time sword fastened to his side by a much worn and faded morocco belt and a large, rusty, brass buckle, a common hat, with a white plume made of goose feathers stuck under a cockade of red, white and blue flannel, and would take his position in front of the company with drawn sword and command, "Attention, company; front face; company rank and size, the tall men to the front and the little men to the left, march."

Then there was some commotion among the privates to find their position. After the company became settled the captain would again command, "Attention, company; front face; look to the right; eyes right." Then all eyes were turned to the right of the company to make the line straight. The captain then had the company go through the manual of arms, commencing, "Order arms, shoulder arms, present arms, support arms, trail arms, prepare to load, draw ramrod, handle cartridge, ram down cartridge, return ramrod, prime, order arms." All this was done in a short space of time, with perhaps only twenty guns in a company of 100 men, and the guns of all kinds and patterns, shapes and forms, from the squirrel rifle to the old war musket and blunderbus with flint locks.

After this performance he would

command the company to "mark time," the captain then taking position in front of and to the extreme right of the company, and under a full flow of martial music he stood calling out, "right foot, left foot, right foot, left foot, right face, march;" then, after countermarching on the same ground, the word was, "halt, mark time." All this seemed interesting, both to the performers and lookers on.

It is remembered in the days of general musters, a company of the "cornstalk militia," as they were called, from one of the rural districts, was formed in the rear of the old court house. The captain commanding was supposed to possess some military knowledge and pride, and strove to infuse some of these desirable accomplishments into the men under his command.

Several ludicrous scenes would sometimes occur in the midst of this mimic war. An awkward fellow, who had been indulging too freely at the village bar, appeared in the ranks at loose ends. The captain, observing his situation and condition, cried out: "Jim Stokes, stand up, there; straighten up and pull up them legs, one foot at the mouth of Salt and the other at the mouth of Meigs Creek, heels together, toes out; attention, company; silence, order in ranks, quit acting the d—d fool; don't you see all this town gentry laughing and making fun of you?" It took some little time to get these noisy, turbulent and awkward fellows into military position according to "Cooper," the military tactics consulted at that day. The company being put in shape, the sergeant stepped to the front and drew forth from under his military jacket the muster roll of the company, and commenced calling over the same; first commissioned and non-commissioned officers, then the privates.

The responses to some of the names when called afforded much merriment to both the men in the ranks and bystanders. The sergeant, having a strong voice and priding himself on the position he held, acted well his part in the military farce going on before him. He commanded the company, "Stand at ease, and attend roll call." Thereupon, some sat down, some laid down in every conceivable and comfortable position they might fancy, and some continued to stand awaiting roll call. The sergeant, with roll in hand and a pin to mark the absentees with a prick, called the name of Peter Stockly, who answered, "I am here." (Not having access at this late day to the muster rolls, we are compelled to supply the names of those who were priced down as absent, with the excuses they produced, as best we can): "Patrick Holden;" "It's me ye are after, I am here, my lord." "Silas Smith;" some one in the ranks, after calling his name three times, as was the rule, cried out: "Prick him down, run off to Vaginney." "Enoch Strong;" "Cut his foot, can't walk." "Simeon Snediker;" "Wife sick." "James Huffmire;" "Prick him down, got no shoes, bare-footed." "Stephen Brownlow;" "Prick him down; got married last inght." "Abraham Lansing;" "Prick him down; too d—d lazy to come." "Jacob Stotle;" "Making sauer kraut." "Peter Stiver;" "Prick him down; joined the 'New Lights'." "Julius Ralston;" "Prick him down; run off to Kanawha salt works." "Saumel Stiles;" "Dodging Nance Smith; prick him down." "Joshua Stonefellow;" "Constable took him to Zanesville for hog stealing; prick him down." "Henry Pettycone;" "Old mare sick." "Quinteus Polenus;" "Prospecting for silver on Salt Creek; prick him down." "William Hawk;" "After his runaway buzzard; prick him down." "Stephen Tinsmith;" "Stole a horse and run off; prick him down." "Shepard Lawson;" "Prick him down; gone west to enter land." "David Judkins;" "Run off to Hard Scrabble with Susan Rightstine; prick him down." "James Conmallen;" "Husking corn; has no bread." "John Brown;" "Got the measles." "Geo.

Cope;" "Got a baby; prick him down. No, no," all along the rank, "Prick him up." "Peter Steinbrock;" "Out of the county; gone to the Devil's Half Acre." "Joab Stevens;" "Very sick at Muttonburg;" and so on to the end of the roll were the absentees burlesqued, excused and accounted for by those present in the ranks.

It was often the case that such scenes as that at "roll call" above related took place among the militia. Many of our people looked upon military demonstrations as of no great importance, and through their opposition they frequently became subject to burlesque and contempt.
First Trading on Orleans Boats, Etc.

In 1825 and along about that period, some of our villagers having a little capital, some credit, and immense enterprise, concluded to do something for themselves, their neighbors and posterity. Joseph McConnell, then a young man, built at our landing a flat, or trading boat. A flat-boat at that day was so called because it had a flat bottom, with no rake at stem or stern.

This kind of boat was about 18 feet wide and from 50 to 80 feet long, built strong and substantial in all its parts, with gunwhales or gunnels from eight to ten inches thick, and as wide as could be gotten out of the poplar trees which then grew to great size here upon the townsite, with studding placed at proper intervals at the sides and ends, and planked up three or four feet constituted the hull or chamber of the boat. This kind of a water craft was known among river men by the appellation of "Orleans boat." Some of these boats, in after days, were built so as to carry from 1200 to 1500 barrels of flour, 1000 barrels of pork, and from 300 to 500 barrels of salt, and a capacity for immense quantities of other products for the lower trade. The use of such boats was the cheapest, and, in fact, the only way our people had of transporting their trade to distant markets, and then only when the waters in the several rivers were found to be in good boating stage. These boats were generally roofed with inch boards reaching from side to side, with suitable pitch from the center so as to dispose of the water that fell and a protection to the cargo; and so arranged that the oarsmen and pilot could safely stand anywhere upon the same in the management of the boat. An "Orleans boat" with a full cargo generally required in its management one or two pilots or steersmen and from four to six oarsmen. In the stern of the boat was the caboose, or cabin, fitted up for cooking, eating and sleeping, and was generally well supplied with substantial but rough provender.

Joseph McConnell's first adventure in the way of boating to New Orleans was in the construction of a rude flat-boat, with but few of the conveniences and advantages that characterized the same kind of boats in after years.

The cargo of this boat consisted entirely of barrel staves and heading, split out in the rough, and stowed away in what was called the hull between studding and plank; no roof, a rough caboose in the stern, with plank on top of the cargo sufficient only for the pilot and oarsmen to stand, walk and work upon in controlling the craft. At the June freshet, for in those days our boatmen always looked for a rise in the river in that month, suitable to carry them to market, McConnell cast off his lines in the presence of an enthusiastic concourse of villagers, who gathered upon our banks to witness the departure of the first adventure of one of its enterprising and most popular citizens. John Alexander, a young, active river man, undertook the pilotage, and the owner and others composed the crew of this, the first "Orleans boat," from the port of McConnelsville. Everything went well with the boat in the Muskingum and Ohio rivers, but, unfortunately, the boat was snagged upon a Mississippi sawyer and all was lost;

that is, the boat and cargo were a total loss, but the officers and crew escaped to relate in after days to their friends and children their trials, difficulties and escapes.

By no means daunted or discouraged at the unfavorable termination of this, his first venture, McConnell, with Jacob R. Price, the spring following, built and loaded two boats with like cargoes of staves and heading, pushed out from our landing, and in due time arrived safe and in good order at their place of destination.

At that day they paid here for staves $5 per M. and sold them on the Mississippi for $20 per M. This trade has long since been abandoned. The Mississippi cyprus has superseded the oak staves of the Muskingum.

In the same spring McConnell and St. Clair built a substantial boat of an entirely different model from that of the stave boat. It was a horse boat. In the middle of the capacious hull was erected a large tread-wheel and this wheel, with horses upon it, was the power by which the boat was propelled. It was in its construction and in all its appointments a kind of rude steamboat, saving and excepting the propelling power. To all observers it was a "nonesuch," and a craft the like of which had never before appeared upon the western waters, and in its voyage down the Muskingum, Ohio and Mississippi rivers was quite a curiosity to the denizens along the banks.

Its cargo was varied and much mixed, being what a supercargo would call "an assorted cargo," consisting in the main of horses and hound dogs. In those days horses of a superior quality were quite scarce, but hound dogs were plenty and cheap. Upon this boat were about 30 horses and 20 pairs of dogs. The horses occupied the hold and lower deck; the dogs were chained in pairs upon the upper deck or roof, and such other kind of produce as the country afforded and which was in demand in the lower trade was the cargo of this water craft. The dogs kept up a discordant music which, together with the horse machinery, made it quite annoying to the voyagers and called the attention and curiosity of people all along the shore. The horses were provided with the usual feed, but cold mush was the diet of the dogs. At this day one may be disposed to wonder and laugh at the idea of trading in dogs, but the fact was, the proprietors made more upon their dog freight, taking all things into consideration, than upon any other part of the cargo.

We shall note some other boating and water-craft reminiscences. We remember that Mr. Jacob Adams loaded at our landing at an early day an Orleans boat with pork adn wheat, and also carried a lot of horses. Maysville, Ky., was the nearest point below here where the wheat could be advantageously manufactured into flour. Wheat was then bought at 30 to 50 cents per bushel, and pork at $2 per hundred net. There were large steam flouring mills at Maysville, and Adams & Co. exchanged their wheat for flour, giving six bushels of wheat for one barrel of flour, and sold the flour in New Orleans for $2.50 and $3.00 per barrel, and got for pork $9 and $9.25. Horses did not prove to be a profitable investment. Sales were slow and the expense of keeping horses very large. To show that times are not what they used to be as to buying and selling horses, we would relate one instance in this horse venture of Adams & Co. A small horse, costing here $22, was exchanged at Baton Rouge with a French planter who was without money but who had plenty of cotton, for two bales. The cotton was sold at New Orleans for 11 cents per pound, realizing about $90. It will be seen that in those days our speculators and traders were content with small profits, though going a great distance to find a market, exchanging, bartering, and bringing home sugar, molasses, cotton and rice of the south instead of money. About those days, and through our traders, New Orleans sugar and molasses were first introduced to our people, and from that time forward became a large and important trade and was sought after at good prices.

Merchants from neighboring villages and distant points came here and bought New Orleans sugars from our southern traders. In after years, and prior to the improvement of the Muskingum, large quantities of salt were manufactured here upon the river which hereabouts to some extent superseded the produce trade down the river. Salt in vast quantities, when navigation proved suitable, was sent to the various towns along the Ohio as low down as the Falls, by salt boats. The salt boat was a rather hard institution to live, move and have an existence upon. It was a craft more uncomfortable, unhandy and unmanageable than was the old stave boat. Salt is a heavy freight and the boat, when laden, sinks deep into the water, requiring several hands to safely manage the craft through the dangers of navigation, particularly at that day upon the Muskingum. A goodly number of these salt boats going off on freshets would meet with losses, accidents and remarkable escapes.

Once upon a time a salt boat, heavy laden and hailing from our village with a well known reverend gentleman as supercargo, and a no less well known river man by the name of Jones, a pilot, came near being cast away in the raging, turbulent, crooked and intricate channel of Luke Chute, at that day a very dangerous place upon the Muskingum. On approaching the dreaded danger, all hands were called to man the sweeps, so as to avoid the same if possible. The Reverend Supercargo, with all others on board, came to the rescue, seized the sweeps, and labored with all their might, skill and strength to keep the boat off the rocks and in the crooked channel. The indefatigable and experienced helmsman, seeing that all danger was about passed, encouragingly called out to his frightened, trembling and swearing oarsmen, "Now give her hell, boys!" Rev. Supercargo, hearing the word of command from the pilot and believing that all would be lost unless the command were obeyed, unthoughtedly took up the expressive command, and in an excited voice repeated to his comrades at the sweeps, "Now give her hell, boys;" then, discovering his mistake and in a lower voice, "as Jones says." All hands claimed and gave the honor of saving the boat, cargo and all on board to the timely recital of the captain's command by the badly frightened supercargo. This was the last trip of the reverend gentleman down the river upon a salt boat, the company, the rough fare and the dangers of navigation forever after deterring him in that direction; besides, there were no bounds to the profanity indulged in by the rough salt boatmen.

This salt at the stores, groceries and all retail places in the country and at all down river markets was called "Zanesville salt," when, in fact, not one-fourth of it was made in or about Zanesville or even in Muskingum county.

Morgan Co. is the great salt manufacturing region in this part of Ohio, and if the article is deserving of a name or local designation it should have been called "Muskingum salt;" but the envy, prejudice and impudence of a few salt speculators of Zanesville in an early day presumed to interfere and be present at the christening.

The erection of flouring mills following the improvement of our river greatly encouraged the growing of wheat in this and adjoining counties. Large quantities of flour made here and at other places upon the river found an easy and cheap shipment in large Orleans boats to New Orleans and thence by ships to all parts of the world—so that the brand of Muskingum flour was popular and sought after in all places. The reputation thus obtained for the Muskingum flour still holds good at this day, but the quantity manufactured has declined more than one-half. The insects, the seasons and other causes combining have greatly diminished the quantity of wheat grown in this part of Ohio. The flour now made here, over and above the demands for home consumption, finds a ready market in the east by means of short water transportation and by railroads constructed within the last 20 or 25 years. These new and more expeditious channels of communication have entirely superseded the long, tedious and dangerous water route to New Orleans, and the occupation of Orleans boatmen and the use of Orleans boats are gone and disappeared forever.

These multifarious changes in the ways and modes of trade and commerce which have been gradually going on during the last 55 years are now scarcely thought of and but little regretted; but all will readily admit that it would be greatly to our advantage if a few links wanting in this great chain of transportation could be supplied and made available to our wants and interests.

Log Cabin and Hewn Log House Era

The American is a progressive individual. He can not nor will he stand still. He will exercise his intellectual faculties and his locomotive powers and move forward. He is equally progressive with any other people in the arts and sciences, in theology and law and in everything favorably presenting itself to his understanding and interest. In ascertaining the best government for man he has shown himself preeminently the superior of any other people. We need not go back more than 60 years here in the western wilds and present the appearance of things at that day, and then let the living of the present day mark the contrast. Three-quarters of a century ago might be found located here in the primeval forests the rude hut occupied by the hunter and trapper. After the peace of 1795, the occupant of the hut was the monarch of the locality, believing himself secure in his assumed position of a squatter. These frontiersmen seemed contented and happy in the enjoyment of the occupation they followed affording to them, by the use of the gun and the trap, ample employment and support. In time came along the settler who, with his "tomahawk right" in the wilderness or certificate of entry, reared his log cabin and settled down permanently, as he thought, not to be disturbed in the enjoyment of his possessions or crowded out by the great tide of emigration flowing into the wilderness after the peace of 1795.

But few of those early pioneers remain among us or are their former habitations to be seen. They are either dead or have followed the trail of the red man toward the setting sun. The present generation knows nothing experimentally of the trials and hardships endured by their fathers and mothers here in Morgan county at an early day.

The cabin was their domicile, their castle and their abiding place for the present. It was a rude structure, built of sizable logs cut down in the immediate vicinity of its location, hauled or rolled to the foundation and put up into house shape by the help of the few neighbors who, in those days, were real neighbors, disinterested and unselfish. These neighbors were "few and far between," but freely would they come to the help of one another when the work called for strong, robust and active men. The cabin was put up in a square form, corners notched down, roofed with clapboards rived out in the forest nearby, secured in place with poles placed at proper distances, and with boalts of wood between to keep them apart and in position. The floor was either earthen or made of puncheons, so-called, split out, hewn, joined and fastened down upon sleepers. No nails were used in those days.

The wooden pin or peg was the pioneer substitute. The rafters and joists of the cabin in the winter and fall seasons were well hung with dried venison, bear and other wild meat, with a large sprinkling of the never ending still beginning links of sausages, unintentionally foreshowing to the stranger and the uninitiated the cabalistic emblem of "Friendship, Love and Truth."

The spaces between the logs were chunked and daubed. The chimneyplace, made of "cat and clay," was immense, and in capacity sufficient to admit firewood of great size—six by two feet back logs, forestick and other wood in proportion were heaped up in the place, and when fully ignited afforded to the family and guests a charming, cheerful and hot fire. Many of the numerous self-made men that the west has produced, took their start in the study of books around the blazing fire of the log cabin. They have distinguished themselves as students in theology, law, politics, and mechanics. Split-bottom chairs, stools, benches, a rough table, antiquated bed-steads, an old chest, a rude cupboard, and a hominy-block, all made from the forest with the ax, composed the principal furniture of the primitive resting place of the pioneer settler. The table furniture consisted of bright and shining pewter plates and platters, conspicuously arranged in the shelves of the rude cupboard, and perhaps two knives and forks, a like number of cups and saucers, for the special use of "Dad and Marm," upon which they ate their wild meat and out of which they drank their spicewood and sassafras teas, and their rye, wheat, and corn coffee. Hands and teeth, being made before knives and forks, sufficed for the children in the disposal of the feast of wild meat, hog and hominy, and corn bread set before them. The most of the time the pioneer and his family lived sumptuously, but there were times of pinching famine.

A wide doorway as an entrance and a loop hole for light were cut out of the sides of the cabin. The door was made of clap-boards, hung on wooden hinges, wooden fastenings, with a tow or leather string attached to the latch hanging upon the outside, saying to the passing neighbor or stranger, "Our latch string is out; you are welcome." The window space was filled with greased paper, which kept out the cold and furnished a tolerably good light.

This cabin in all its appointments was of the rudest kind, where cheerfulness and contentment seemed to dwell, but those who were "richer" (in fact, in domestic conveniences, all were very poor), could afford something better.

Such habitations were occupied until the settler cleared up and improved his claim, and until he became better off in worldly goods, with his cabin house full of children —then it was that the pioneer, from necessity and perhaps pride, was urged to pick out a new site for a larger and more convenient domicile.

The pioneer progresses from the rude log cabin to the erection of a hewn log house. This house may be a story and a half or two stories, brick or stone chimney, shingle or clapboard roof put on with nails, brought from Wheeling or Pittsburg, the spaces between the logs filled in with white lime mortar which, when dry, made a fine appearance—glass windows, a cellar, battened or panel doors, cabinet furniture, blue or variegated Liverpool cupboard-ware, and other table and household conveniences required and introduced by the times.

We have thus attempted to describe the log cabin and hewn log house eras in pioneer life. Whatever omissions are made will perhaps be found unimportant and may be supplied by the reader. The next and last step taken in this work of progress and improvement is the erection of a fine, commodious and well furnished brick or frame dwelling in the vicinity or upon the foundation of where stood the old houses. These modern structures may now be seen dotting the country all over, in the valleys and upon the hill tops, well furnished, well located and convenient in all things.

The old log cabin, like "the old oaken bucket, the iron bound bucket, the moss covered bucket" that once hung in the well, has disappeared, and is only remembered in song, whilst the old hewn log house is now a waste or the habitation of owls and bats.

There are still among us those who can remember the log cabin era in Morgan county, when almost everything consumed by the settler and family was raised upon his clearing or obtained by the chase. In those days there was some barter with the trader. Skins and furs were exchanged for coffee and tea, which were luxuries, kept snug away out of sight and brought forth in case of sickness or when the itinerant minister or a visitor would come along, or a wedding should happen. What little wool was then shorn and carded, spun, and woven by hand was made into linsey-woolsey fabrics and worked up into clothing for the family. Flax was then cultivated and went from the field into the break, and from the break to the hatchel and loom, where it was manufactured into tow-linen, out of which were made the shirts and pantaloons of the men folks. The deer skin and cow skin were sometimes tanned at home, and from the home-tanned leather, shoes and moccasins were made.

The implements then used in the cultivation of the soil were of the rudest and simplest kind. The farmer boy of the present day does not fully comprehend or know the use of the old pioneer grain sickle. He can wield with skill the grain cradle or drive the reaper and cut and gather the grain in half the time consumed by our pioneer fathers and at much less cost. The grain was threshed out with the flail or tramped out with horses. The one horse power endless chain threshing machine and piano made their advent here in Morgan county at about the same time and both were held as extravagant innovations, and knowing ones would predict that they would likely break their owners. The world still moves along notwithstanding the predictions of the old fogies. Improved threshing machines, reapers, mowers, and all kinds of musical instruments are found upon the farm and in the parlors of the farm houses, attesting that they have kept up with the progress of the ages that neither can or will be dispensed with.

Our village in the primitive days, 54 years ago, had scattered, here and there over the first survey of lots, the log cabin. A few hewn log houses and perhaps one brick and one frame house might be seen. The school house was a log cabin structure, decidedly uncouth without and rough within. It was the Town House, where all public meetings were held, before the building of the first or old court house. The old court house was a free institution open to all and for every purpose: courts, elections, religious meetings of all denominations, and all kinds of shows at all times found the old court house free and open to them. Though never dedicated, the Methodist, the pioneer church here in the wilderness; the Presbyterians, Baptists, and all other denominations of christians generally worshipped in the old court house, and that, too, without clashing or discord. This state of affairs continued until first the Baptists, then the Presbyterians, and then the Methodists, swarmed from the old court house into new church edifices.

One of these original church buildings is in existence, the Baptist was burned down some years since and the congregation has been wandering here and there until recently they have erected, finished and paid for one of the best and neatest church buildings in the county. The old stone church of the Methodist denomination, "Old Brimstone," as it was called, has given way to the present large and very convenient structure. Our village is now well supplied with large, convenient, neat and substantial meeting houses, where almost all christian denominations now extant may worship. No longer does the old court house, the old log cabin school house, and the private dwellings hear the voice of a McElroy, Ruckel, Culbertson, Hunt, Plumstead, Elder, George Russell, and others, soldiers of the cross and pioneering ministers of the gospel in McConnelsville. They are "gone, all silent and all hushed up."

(THE END)

www.ingramcontent.com/pod-product-compliance
Lightning Source LLC
Chambersburg PA
CBHW030349100526
44592CB00010B/886